Praise for
FINALLY THE BRIDE

"You know how in a romantic comedy, the girl gets the guy in about one hour and forty minutes? If that's not your story, this book is for you. Cheryl has turned her journey of pain, rejection, and the endless wait for a soul mate into a book filled with humor, rawness, sometimes hard-to-swallow truth, and most of all, hope. Whether you're waiting on true love or waiting for God to answer your most important prayer, come along with Cheryl and you'll feel less alone and more empowered to wait at the feet of a Savior who dearly loves you. By the end of it all, you'll gladly 'surrender the pen.' *Finally the Bride* is a beautiful account of a girl chasing a guy and God chasing the girl."

--**Rene Gutteridge**, Author, *My Life as a Doormat*, Co-Author, *Never the Bride*

"Starved for a soul mate? Follow McKay's breadcrumbs along this very personal journey of faith. This is no light confection of a book. Frankly witty and achingly raw, it is written out of first-hand experience by a woman who choked down one rejection after another, year after bewildering year. It's about turning to God for heart-level sustenance through extended lean seasons, and the romantic feast she discovered at long last, waiting at the table of her First Love."

--**Susan Rohrer**, Author, *THE HOLY SPIRIT: Amazing Power for Everyday People, IS GOD SAYING HE'S THE ONE: Hearing from Heaven about That Man in Your Life*

"We met right after high school, dated throughout college, and had the blessing of being married in our early twenties. This allowed us to almost grow up together and begin pursuing our calling as a couple. Other people, like Cheryl, find purpose during many years of singleness while waiting for that much-desired walk down the aisle. Cheryl is a gifted writer who brings a great perspective to anyone seeking to find the right spouse or have a great marriage."

--**Crystal Stovall**, Author, *A Groom Worth Waiting For* & **Jim Stovall**, Author, *The Ultimate Gift*

"Cheryl's willingness to be vulnerable and share the personal, sometimes painful, lessons of faith, learned as a single Christian woman wrestling with God's timing and perfect plan for her life, brings such hope and encouragement to those in their own season of waiting. You are not alone. Here is someone who gets it, who has lived it, and offers practical tips and wise advice from her own experience. Cheryl's words bring laughter, tears, and a reminder of truth: that God is for us, His plans are good and perfect, and He is trustworthy to use the pain and joy of our lives to write a beautiful story, if only we will surrender the pen."

> --**Christa Sands**, Author, *Learning to Trust Again*

"With courageous transparency, Cheryl invites us to share her journey of faith as she waits on God to write her love story. Sometimes hilarious, sometimes heartbreaking, the path is not a smooth or easy one. Cheryl lays bare her heart as she expresses her frustration, mistakes, joys, and victories. And through it all, her fierce pursuit of her Lord and His will alone shines through. The words she received from the Lord in her journal are rich with wisdom that will resonate with all of us who have waited longer than we expected for God's promises to be fulfilled. Funny. Honest. Wise. Not just a book for singles, every Christian can grow and be blessed by the truths Cheryl has learned."

> --**Mark & Patti Virkler**, Authors, 4 *Keys to Hearing God's Voice, Counseled by God, Prayers that Heal the Heart, Rivers of Grace*

"*Finally the Bride* is a wonderfully warm, vulnerable, and frank illustration of what it means to let God write your love story, and what it is to have a love story with God. McKay offers practical, and often humorous, advice on not getting sidetracked from the ultimate goal of letting God be the only One in your life to chose the one for your life. As Cheryl reveals her very personal triumphs and failures in her struggle to be patient, she emphasizes the importance of not getting stuck in the desperation of waiting and wanting. She encourages the single person who believes they are to be married, to live life fully in the waiting—to enjoy the time with God and learn what it means to be fully committed to Him, before being committed to a different 'him.'"

> --**Caroline Way**, Author, *Confessions From a Farmer's Wife*

Finally
the
Bride

Finding Hope While Waiting

By Cheryl McKay

By Cheryl McKay

Never the Bride (screenplay)
Never the Bride a novel (with Rene Gutteridge)
The Ultimate Gift (screenplay)
The Ultimate Life (screenplay)
Gigi: God's Little Princess DVD (screenplay)
Wild & Wacky, Totally True Bible Stories Series
(with Frank Peretti)

Coming Soon:

Finally Fearless: Journey from Panic to Peace
Greetings from the Flipside a novel (with Rene Gutteridge)

Finally the Bride:
Finding Hope While Waiting

Cover image by Lisa Crates Photography/lisacrates.us
Additional images by Christopher Price
Purple PenWorks Artwork by Heather Gebbia

All scripture quotations, unless otherwise indicated, are taken from the Holy
Bible, New International Version®, NIV®. Copyright ©1973, 1978, 1984, 2011
by Biblica, Inc.™ Used by permission of Zondervan. All rights reserved
worldwide. www.zondervan.com
The "NIV" and "New International Version" are trademarks registered in the
United States Patent and Trademark Office by Biblica, Inc.™

Additional scripture quotations are from:
The Holy Bible, King James Version (KJV). Public Domain.

God Winks® is a registered trademark of SQuire Rushnell.

Appendix of God-Written Love Stories used by permission of the individual
authors. Copyrights are held by the original authors.

ISBN-13: 978-1470005931
ISBN-10: 147000593X
Copyright © 2012 by Cheryl McKay
Published in the United States of America
2012 — First Edition

For those who are weary
in their wait to find
true love

TABLE OF CONTENTS

CHAPTER ONE

Introducing the Impatient One

> *MISSING:*
> *My husband.*
> *He's tall. He's dark. He's handsome.*
> *I think. Actually, I don't know. I may not have met him yet.*
> *He could be a short, balding blond with a dimpled cheek. If*
> *you find him, please call me at 1-777-HUSBAND. Reward*
> *offered. If you are that guy – the one who hasn't shown up*
> *yet – your M.I.A. nature is completely unacceptable to your*
> *future wife.*

Everyone has a diagnosis for me:

Why I'm in my thirties and still single.

Did you hear I'm still single because God hasn't finished preparing me yet? Yes, in thirty-something years, I haven't managed to become mature enough for marriage. Don't worry. It gets better. Apparently, I'm still single because I *want* to be married. If only I didn't want it, then I could have it. I've seen many knuckleheads get married, much younger than I am. You can't tell me they were more prepared! I don't want to talk about how every kid I ever babysat is now married, already popping out babies in need of a sitter. Seriously. I don't want to talk about it!

Have your friends and family offered opinions about why you're still single, as though you have some defect that must be fixed before you are worthy of someone's love? (I wanted to temporarily maim those people, too.)

If you have been waiting for God to introduce you to the love of your life, travel with me on a voyage through the ups and downs of singleness.

My desire for anyone reading this book is for you to find hope. We are about to embark on a journey, one that can show you and me why we can be hopeful while we are single. I want you to see that you are absolutely okay, that God cares about your love life and your heart, and that you can have a strong sense of what you are supposed to do with yourself while you wait. Oh, and did I mention the best thing you can do while waiting is fall in love with God?

Falling in love with God is much like enlisting in Marriage Boot Camp. Now, I am not suggesting you sign up for this Boot Camp because I think you need a lot more preparation before you're worthy of love and marriage. However, if you're like me, you have nothing better to do while waiting for that "in the flesh" husband to arrive. At your doorstep. Sporting a bow. (Like a Christmas bow because anything else would be creepy.) You might as well make the most of the time and learn all you can from being in a true love relationship with God. He's the One you're going to want to still be in love with even after you get married. Maybe we'll need God's help to still love and accept our husbands when they leave dirty boxers strewn on the floor!

Right before I got the idea for this book, a friend said to me in that prophetic sense, "God is about to give you a new idea to write." Considering I write movies, I assumed she meant a script. Within a couple of days, the idea for this book, *Finally the Bride*, hit me.

My first reaction was, "No way! Huh-uh! God, if launching into writing this book is yet another reason for You to keep me single longer—so I get to expand my ministry base to help the 'I'm Still Single and Waiting Crowd' — no, thank you. Forget it!"

I resisted the idea, too, because I wanted to write about something else. Like, how about a book on the first year of marriage? Well, it's best that I write what I know and, friends, I know nothing about surviving the first year of marriage.

My moaning continued: "God, I've been writing about my singleness through scripts, stories, other books, articles, blogs, every format imaginable. When do my stories get to change?" My whining did not sway God; the inspiration kept coming. I sensed this was one of God's assignments for me, despite my protests. Then I went to a prayer meeting where this man I didn't know came up to me and said I'd write a new book to help other people. "Okay, fine, Lord. I get your point. You want me to help other people." *Grrr.*

Yes, I am a brat sometimes, but I also feel this is a message to which other people are bound to relate. I wasn't exactly filling up my schedule with dates. So, why not? What's to say that by the time I finish this book, its title, *Finally the Bride*, won't have a dual meaning? Not just finally the bride of Christ, but also, finally a real flesh-and-blood bride in a real white dress — because at this point I still qualify to wear one. (Yes, I am well on my way to becoming the 40-year-old virgin. That is *not* a title I'm hoping to win. "Did you hear that, God? I have deadlines. So far, you've blown them all. Please, don't blow this one!")

Throughout this book, you will hear me reference when people have offered prophetic words to me, or times I've felt God has spoken directly to me. I do believe God still speaks today. I believe His heart's desire is to be involved in our lives. If He didn't speak or reach out to us in tangible ways, how could we be in the love relationship with Him that He says He craves with us in His Word?

This isn't the place to explore the theology behind why I believe God speaks. I just want to set the stage that you will often hear me reference God speaking. (If you have no idea how to hear God's voice, I suggest you read Mark and Patti Virkler's book, *4 Keys to Hearing God's*

Voice. Do a study of Scriptures that back up what they teach.)

In this book, my prayer journaling includes conversations with God. Please note: If any error exists in my journal entries, grammatically or content wise, I take full responsibility. Hearing God correctly is not based on some formula. I could make mistakes. Also, sometimes what I'm sensing comes faster than I can possibly write. So, I may miss words or phrases here and there and have to capture the essence of what I feel God is speaking.

I'll include some of my most honest journal entries, even though some embarrass me. (I can be quite a moan-head!) If you're in my boat, you'll relate to what I have to say about this. To you. To God. To anyone who's listening. I'll also show you some words I feel God spoke back to me, to encourage my spirit during times of despair or when I needed a reality check, a reminder that life isn't all about me or my future mate!

I will also share other people's God-written love stories at the end of this book. They are the types of stories that have encouraged me to see that God does this for people, even if it hasn't happened yet in my own life.

So, are you ready? Do you want God to write your love story?

> *Dear God:*
>
> *You said in Your Word that man is not meant to be alone. Seriously. You can look it up in Genesis 2:18. So, why do You insist I remain alone? Okay, so I realize I'm not a man. However, I think the spirit behind what You said about Adam included women. After all, when You didn't want Adam to be alone, You created Eve. Did You know, when You said those words, many singles would throw them back in Your face in moments of frustrated isolation?*
>
> *— Sincerely,*
> *Your Lonely Daughter Cheryl*

CHAPTER TWO
Seriously! Why Would God Care About My Love Life?

> ### TO DO LIST:
> #### (Things Cheryl Must Do Before She Can Get Married)
>
> 1. Write a book about her contentedness at being single (and try not to lie too much).
> 2. Learn how to cook more than grilled chicken salad and vegetable soup.
> 3. Start separating her lights and darks when she does laundry.
> 4. Recognize that undergarments with holes not meant for sex appeal should be thrown away.
> 5. Stop rolling her eyes every time a lovey-dovey couple walks by holding hands.
>
> *List to be continued...*

I sat in the middle of the kitchen floor.

Crying.

Over pickles.

I couldn't get the gallon jar of vinegar-soaked cucumbers open so I could add them to my salad. (You can't have a good salad in my world without tangy pickles!) I thought to *myself*—because no one else was there to listen—*Why is the world and this stupid jar against me?!* Then, my disapproving-self chimed in: *Cheryl, you are crying over pickles. In case you didn't know, you're an idiot!*

At the same time, I understood the real reason for my tears. It wasn't about food; I was alone. I was tired of being alone. There should have been a guy there to rescue me and open the pain-provoking pickle jar. Yet, no amount of prayers produced a jar-opening dude.

Lord, why am I still alone?

Silence.

That is not rhetorical and yet, every time I ask, You are noticeably silent.

My roommate at the time—another "single and waiting too long" woman like me—bought a jar opener for my birthday that year.

So, I no longer needed the man.

That episode has since been coined "The Pickle Jar Moment." I now live alone, but my former roommate and I still call each other up and say, "I had a Pickle Jar Moment today." We proceed to share some story from the day that made us feel acutely single.

God? An Author of Love Stories?

Did you know that God wants to write our love stories for us? Have you heard of this concept? Isn't that a bold statement coming from the woman He clearly hasn't done it for yet? If He had, you can bet I would have lost interest in writing this book! I would have moved on to other topics: marriage, maybe even motherhood.

I guess this is where faith steps in, faith in the midst of no tangible evidence (Hebrews 11:1). I know what you're thinking: *Doesn't God have better things to do like solving world hunger, the ozone problem, peace, and scads of issues the other seven billion people on this planet face?* Yes, but that's where His omniscience (all-knowingness) and omnipresence (being everywhere) comes in handy. God actually can assist me with my love life while helping a third world country.

God *is* love. As the creator of love and marriage, He does care. He is the One who designed the marital relationship. (Newsflash: He even created sex!) As I mentioned before, He's the one who judged that man should not live alone. Of course, He cares about the decision I hope I will only have to make once in my lifetime.

Being a writer, I have a wildly active imagination. Many pages of my journals have been filled with words about my future love life (with my trusty, purple feathered pen). However, do those words and hopes leave those pages and walk into my reality?

Not so far.

Seriously. Not even one.

So, where did I get this idea that God wants to do this for us? Well, from God Himself, on a lonely February day. I was just beginning to get over a relationship I thought had been leading toward marriage. This is what I felt God said to me:

> *Cheryl's Journal (February 10, 2004)*
> *"My tender Cheryl, let Me love you for a while. Make Me enough. Your love is coming. He is coming. Put it aside for now and wait on Me. You will watch My faithfulness unfold. You have plenty to focus on right now. It will sneak up on you when you least expect it. Lay it all down. I have given you plenty of tasks. Focus on those. Let Me pave the way for your love story. You don't need to do anything. Let Me write your love story. Let Me be the Author."*

I had been through enough bad relationships. Letting God take over sounded like the biggest relief, even for a control freak like me.

That was 2004.

Not exactly the whirlwind romance, huh? I'm a much faster writer than God, apparently. And what's this about how it will sneak up on me when I least expect it? Seriously! Don't even get me started on that comment! I expected it a long time ago. (I am a relentless hoper.) That's when the metaphors began: God as a scriptwriter, God's script pages, God's storyline, God's mystery casting, God's special pen. The pen I occasionally want to snatch back when He isn't writing fast enough or when He writes words I'd rather edit out like "wait" and "delay" and "not now, My impatient one."

I knew I'd be writing a book to share with the world about how God did this for me. I wistfully dreamed of naming it *When God Writes Your Love Story*. One day, I got my confirmation that He does indeed work this way. Perhaps it's more accurate to call it my rude awakening. Apparently, He doesn't just want to do this for me alone.

It was Christmas 2004, about eleven months after that journal entry and almost a year's worth of hearing God speak in story-writing metaphors. I went to a bookstore with my parents. I walked down the aisle of books (not to be confused with the aisle of a church, heading toward some wonderful man. See? I am a hopeless romantic.) A certain book caught my eye. It nearly screamed at me to pick it up. Its title was: *When God Writes Your Love Story*

I wanted to throw it across the store and yell, "They have my title!" The book, which I had never heard of, was written by Eric and Leslie Ludy, a lovely couple who have a ministry to young people. The book encourages readers to wait for God's best, for God's chosen person for marriage, but at that moment, I didn't care about their ministry. I felt annoyed.

I questioned God: "You do this for other people?" (As if I had the market cornered on God and love stories!) I walked away, determined not to buy the book.

God whispered to my frustrated spirit, "You are not leaving that book on the shelf." Curiosity got the best of me, and I opened the book—though I hid it once when my dad walked by.

I was drawn immediately to one segment Leslie wrote of words God had spoken to her about being the author of love, and promising to write her a beautiful, love story script if she'd surrender the pen.

I was stunned. God had practically said those exact words to me almost a year earlier. There I was, reading them in someone else's book.

After my annoyance subsided, I found it encouraging. It showed me that God does indeed speak to me. The same God who made those promises to me—that He would write my love story if only I would surrender the pen—is the same God who promised and *then delivered* love to Leslie. God had the promise part down in my life; the delivery part was M.I.A.

I bought the Ludys' book (and its sequel, *When Dreams Come True*) and devoured them both in days. I found a striking amount of similarities between the journey God had me on and the journey God led Eric and Leslie through. In an ironic twist, they got married on my birthday.

I won't complain too much about how they were a lot younger than I currently am—and I am still waiting. I wanted to have a little chat with Leslie when she complained about the years she had to wait to walk down the aisle once she knew she was going to marry Eric. Part of that time, she was still in high school. I wanted to share with her what waiting feels like when you're in your late thirties. She's been married since 1994, and she's four years younger than I am. God had a specific plan for their lives, using their love story to reach hundreds of thousands of young people. Getting married young was part of that plan. That just wasn't God's script for my life. He was ignoring my rewrite suggestions for do-overs, backing up time, starting my love life years ago.

God's Promises

Has God spoken to you about this area of your life—directly or through other people? Do you have a record of it? If you haven't yet, I encourage you to start a journal. Keep track of all the words, pictures, promises, and encouragement God gives you about your future love story. You can use it to help yourself through seasons of discouragement, to remind yourself of what God has promised. Later, it will be a record of your love story. All phases of our stories—even before love tangibly shows up—are part of the grand tapestry God weaves with our lives.

I shared with you one journal entry in which God asked me to let Him be the Author. I have more reasons to know God has marriage in mind for me. One time, when the promise of a husband came up, it accompanied the delivery of bad news.

In 2003, I thought I was dating the man I was going to marry.

I was wrong.

In a prayer meeting, God gave a woman prophetic words for me: the relationship was about to end. God, as my loving Father, wanted to prepare me before it happened. This warning came one week before it ended. While it was devastating to me, I was so thankful God warned me.

During this same prayer meeting, God didn't just deliver bad news. Because He didn't want me to lose heart—and He could foresee the intensely painful road I had ahead of me—He also delivered the message that I would one day get married. He was taking care of this part of my life for me. God knew I needed that promise to hold on to because the next year became one of the darkest years I've lived.

To this day, I'm still grateful for that promise, even though God has yet to deliver on it. As I read the Bible, I'm in good company. Abraham had to wait twenty-five years for God's promise of a son.

Is There a Precedent for God Setting up Love Matches?

You may be asking what's the precedent that God would write our love stories. Is it just coincidental that I felt God say those words to me, only to find out He did the same for Eric and Leslie Ludy? Let's go straight to the Bible and see. Does God arrange marriages? Does He write love stories? I found in His Word that He does.

Let's explore one example: Isaac and Rebekah. God employs a method of confirmation called "God Winks." A God Wink is a moment when you feel, without a doubt, that God spoke to you or confirmed something in a tangible way, often through something others may consider just a coincidence. (My friend and author, SQuire Rushnell, has an excellent book series called *When God Winks* about such encounters with God. He and his wife share their God-written love story in the appendix of this book.) In later chapters, I will share humorous examples of God using this confirmation method with me. First, let's look at Genesis 24 as an example of a God-written love story.

God made a promise to Abraham that he would be the father of many nations. This was fulfilled through the family lines of Abraham, Isaac, and Jacob, Isaac being the promised heir. For Isaac to do his part in continuing the family line, he had to get married and have children.

Abraham asked his servant, Eliezer, to go out and find a wife for Isaac from his father's family in a specific place. He gave instructions that included a prophecy. Abraham said, "…he will send his angel before you so that you can get a wife for my son from there." (Genesis 24:7b.)

After the servant left on his trip in search of this "mystery wife" for Isaac, he did the right thing: he prayed. "Then he prayed, 'LORD, God of my master Abraham, make me successful today, and show kindness to my master Abraham.'" (Genesis 24:12.) He asked God to give him a specific sign about whom the right woman was. He requested that when he asked for water, the right girl would offer water to him *and* his camels. This would be his signal (or God Wink). I love how verse 15 mentions before he finished praying, Rebekah came out with her jar on her shoulder. I don't know about you, but God doesn't usually answer my prayers before I'm done praying them. When the servant asked for a drink, she gave it to him. Then, she volunteered to get water for his camels, too. (Genesis 24:19.)

Ding, ding, ding. Signal. God Wink.

Eliezer questioned to see if she happened to be from Abraham's father's family, as Abraham had mentioned. Of course, she was! Rebekah was the right young lady. When God matches it up, it's easy to tell, especially when the right time arrives. The servant was ecstatic that he had been led directly to the right woman on Isaac's behalf. He told Rebekah and her family about these signs. He credited God for leading him down the right path. (Genesis 24:23-51.)

Isn't that interesting? We want the right love story, don't we? We don't want to be misled. We don't want detours or wrong turns. We want the one who is right, God's chosen. I love to see how in God's Word, He made it clear that He can write love stories. The precedent was set long ago.

Rebekah's family didn't argue with the servant. They believed this love story was God-written and the union of Rebekah and Isaac was God's will. I realize that doesn't exactly sound like passionate romance. Personally, if I were able to walk into a relationship that I had no doubt God had set up, I believe true love would follow.

Rebekah's response to the call was simple: "I will go." (Genesis 24:58b.) Sight unseen. (I have to wonder what she was thinking at that moment!) I love how Rebekah was enjoying a normal day when God's next purpose for her life arrived. It's likely she didn't see it coming. Her life changed in moments, just like ours can. One day, we feel like we're caught in the mundane routine of life, and the next day, God's destiny shows up and changes everything. (Hmm. Destiny anyone? God? Are you listening? Next day service would be nice.)

Toward the end of Genesis 24, Isaac sees Rebekah for the first time. Their eyes connect; their love story begins.

Rebekah had a choice to make, and she chose rightly. She could have said, "No, I won't go." Instead, she chose the man God ordained for her life. Their marriage wasn't perfect, but lack of perfection doesn't change that her marriage was arranged and put together by God.

Other God-ordained love stories include Adam and Eve, Mary and Joseph, Ruth and Boaz, Esther and King Xerxes. Not all of God's love stories are about romance. They're not always first marriages either. Women who are divorced or widowed shouldn't lose hope. Just keep the pen in God's hands.

Surrendering the Pen to God

Cheryl's Journal (June 18, 1994)

Cheryl's prayer: There must be a reason, Lord, that You want me alone. You must be shaping me for something. I'll be honest. I'm sick of it, but as I always say, You know best. I know it will be special when You, my Lord, finally bless me with marriage and a family. My future is in Your hands. Lord, I don't know where it's headed, but I'd like for You to use me for Your sake and glory.

God's reply: Trust in Me. Take it day by day. Trust that I know what I'm doing. Be patient. Place your security in Me, not in others. Know who you are, firmly grounded in Me first. Then you are free to share your life with someone else. It's a gift. I am the Creator of love. I don't always work in ways expected. Stay open. Receive from Me what I have for you.

Cheryl's prayer: It's not worth accepting a gift from You, God, if I lose You and me in that gift.

God's reply: Your desire is a natural desire. Yet, like everything else, it must fall into place by My timing, not yours.

I was in my early twenties when that conversation with God took place. I had no clue of the path He had planned for me, one characterized so far by all these years of waiting. Even now, this much later, I still believe He knows what's best. It's the only explanation for the grace I've had to walk through many years and trials, without a mate, when my desire for one has been so high.

In my screenwriting profession, there's a timely manner in which script drafts must be completed and turned in. God doesn't seem too interested in my love story script deadlines. If I were writing this script, the dialogue between God and me would go something like this:

God: Cheryl, it's time.
Cheryl: Yippee! I get to switch from "Never the Bride" *to* "Finally the Bride."

I know God cares. I know God is at work, even if I can't see it.

God is at work in your life, too. If I didn't believe that, I wouldn't be sharing this message. There are some people, I realize, who may not be called to marriage. I can't say with certainty that every person who wants to be married will be. Only God knows what He intends for each of us. That's one reason I encourage you to seek confirmation and keep a record of what God reveals about this question.

The Apostle Paul encourages us in 1 Corinthians 7, if we can take it, to stay away from marriage and be sold out to working for God as a single person. Paul acknowledges we are not all called to that lifestyle. I don't believe I am. I do feel God has planned marriage for me in the future. (God, how about tomorrow? If you need a little more time, how about next Wednesday?)

Perhaps you, just like me, don't feel you were meant to be single your whole life. If you're single again through divorce or the death of a spouse, maybe you don't feel like you are to remain single. If that's the case, as you read this book, actively let God take over this part of your life. It is an *action.* Surrender is a daily act and decision. Let God write your love story. No matter how tempting it gets, don't wrestle the pen back or try to borrow it for a few minutes to pen your own storyline!

Before moving on to the next chapter, I'll share with you a funny correction dream God sent at a time when I was trying to yank the pen back from Him.

Dream Story: I'm in a dance studio, waltzing with a guy. A cute guy. I kind of like him. I already know he's not God's choice for me. I'm supposed to be in the other room on a film shoot with the director, acting as his script supervisor. Script supervisors do not write. Their job is to sit by the director and take notes about everything he's putting on film based on a script that's already written. That's it! Track the script, not rewrite it!

I know it's getting close to shooting time and yet I'm in the dance studio, distracted by this guy. He hands me several love notes. I'm caught up in reading them, enjoying his declaration of interest in me. Then I'm called away to the set because shooting is about to start. I'd rather stay with the guy, but I have a job to do. I rush into the room where the scene being filmed stars two lovebirds. I see the director, poised, ready to shoot, and I realize I'm not ready to track this scene or do my job because my copy of the script is somewhere else. I don't know where. My brain is somewhere else, too. I frantically run around trying to get ready, but there's no waiting for me. On set, a director is not going to wait for his script supervisor to be ready. I feel awful, unprepared, and mad at myself for not being where I was supposed to be.

It doesn't take much to decipher what this dream is about, does it? God is the director; I am the script supervisor. I can track what He's doing, in my journals and in books. I am not the writer. I need to be prepared, by His side, waiting for the love story He will write and direct. If I'm too distracted by my own interests and the wrong men, I'll be in the wrong place when He wants to call "action" and unfold my true love story.

When I woke up, this dream made me laugh. It quickly set me back on course, waiting at God's side, ready to see what He wants to do. I enjoy God's loving, even humorous correction sometimes! I do find it ironically hilarious that God made me a writer, and yet, He won't let me write one word of my own love story! Every day I pen adventurous love stories for characters; I control the pen, the outcome. But not in my own life!

I firmly believe, if God has marriage in mind for you, that He wants to write your love story, too. It all starts with the first step: surrendering the pen. Will you surrender that pen, wait by His side, and see what story will unfold before your eyes?

WHAT DOES IT MEAN TO
SURRENDER THE PEN TO GOD?

1. *I must surrender control to God.*
2. *God doesn't want me fantasizing about what He is writing.*
3. *He doesn't want my continuous suggestions.*
4. *He doesn't want me to go off script.*
5. *God wants to keep that pen, and He doesn't want me to try to grab it back every time I fear He might not write what I want. (No tug-of-war games!)*
6. *He doesn't want me to try to influence what He's writing each time I meet a new guy.*
7. *It means I become a player in God's story. I am the actress; He is the writer, director, and executive producer.*
8. *Surrender means trusting Him.*

CHAPTER THREE

Just How Good of a Writer is God?
(Doesn't He Need My Suggestions?)

"THE LIST"
Disclaimer: The following has not been written by, nor inspired by, God the Matchmaker.
Written by: Cheryl McKay (at 14 years old)

1. *A guy who likes to wear socks to bed because I hate feet.*
2. *A guy who looks like he could be my brother, so when we have kids, we'll all look like we belong together.*
3. *A guy who's tall or at least taller than me.*
4. *A guy who's cute.*
5. *A guy who wants daughters.*

Superficiality.

Well, what can we expect from a 14-year-old who has no idea what it means to be married or what she should be looking for? The list back then was longer. It's just funny to see a slice of the traits I used to find important enough to pray for, write down, memorize, laminate.

Have you ever made a list of what you're hoping to find in a husband? If we surrender our love stories to God to write, where does that leave our lists? How do we know God is going to deliver the type of man we want? It's admittedly a bit scary to trust, to place that pen in God's hands and allow Him to take over the writing. What if His opinion for what I need completely differs from my desires? What if the guy He's chosen doesn't even come close to matching the list I've dreamed about my entire life?

I have made many lists then rewritten them, updated them, made additions (especially after bad dates), inserted appendices, qualifications, and disclaimers. I still have a list, but now it bears the official stamp of approval of three prayer mentors. Many of my prior lists would have prompted them to race for the nearest shredder. Often, we want traits we shouldn't use as a basis for acceptance or rejection. Now my list is honed to the most important qualities I desire, and my prayer mentors are open to praying for these traits for me. While I feel most of what I want would line up with God's desires for me, I am open to Him knowing best what I truly need. I have written my list, but He now has custody of the pen and can make His own edits, revisions, insertions, and deletions.

The Pitter-Patter of Desire

Desire is a key word. Most people know the famous verse from Psalm 37:4: "Take delight in the LORD, and he will give you the desires of your heart."

Such a lovely verse, isn't it? If I delight myself in God, He'll hand over *everything* my little heart desires, right? Not really. If this interpretation were true, I would have a car that's less than sixteen years old with power steering and a sunroof. I'd have movie-writing jobs lined up for the next decade, a husband, a child or two, a house with a sweet little porch swing. Oh, and I'd have a baby grand piano in front of the bay window. I want the superpower to travel in the blink of an eye from the West to the East Coast so I could have dinner with my family and be back in my own bed by 11:00 p.m. Psalm 37:4 is the verse I hear misinterpreted the most. People quote it as if God will give us whatever we want if we just delight in Him. That's not what I feel like it says.

If we delight in God, which implies we have a close relationship with Him (enjoying His company, finding joy in that relationship), then I believe He will put the right desires in our hearts. We have a tendency to develop desires that are not best for us. As we grow closer to God, what we desire is more likely to line up with what He wants for us because He helps us hunger for the right things. Those are the desires He tends to fulfill. Yet, it's still in His timing, not ours, even when we desire the right things.

Time has proven to me that Psalm 37:4 does not mean God gives us whatever we want. I often find myself praying for an appetite change. Sometimes, I can tell when my desires are off, when my flesh aches for something God doesn't want for me. The wrong desires don't automatically go away. (Just try breaking an addiction to dark chocolate with a 60% or higher cacao rating!) The more time I spend in communication with God, the easier it is for my desires to line up with His will.

So, what does this have to do with our love lives? I often pray for God to give me the desire for the right man and the right qualities that God wants me to commit to for the rest of my life. How often do we want men who are not good for us? How often do we want a man based on his external looks rather than his heart?

I have been overlooked many times by men—including godly Christian men—because I don't fit a physical profile. They may be looking for a quality that has nothing to do with what's right for them.

Once, when I felt led by God into a relationship to a man I wasn't attracted to, I prayed for God to fix that. My prayer worked. I had an experience one night where it felt like scales fell off my eyes. This man went from not appealing to attractive in one second. I knew, for a season, it was God's will for me to date that person. God had a lot He wanted to teach me about relationships through that one. But let's admit: it helps if attraction plays a role. It just can't be the sole basis for a relationship, when you consider our looks might go sagging downhill as we age. (God, seriously! What were You thinking when You designed us to sag, develop cottage-cheese thighs, and gray hair?) God giving me an attraction for that man was a great example of when I needed God's desires grafted into my heart. He did it! He was able to because I was open to His will above my own. I knew God had a purpose, even though it wasn't my personal preference.

Write That List

I want to encourage you, if you haven't done so already, *prayerfully* write a list. Now, you're not taking over the pen from God. I want you to pray that He reveal to you the qualities you should be looking for in a mate.

You can use this when other guys show up to distract you from the love story God is writing. When one of those comes along and he doesn't match what you feel God has for you, pray that God will show you if the guy is a counterfeit. You don't want to waste your time and your heart on the wrong man, do you?

Come up with everything you think is important to find in a mate. Perhaps it's more accurate to say everything you hope God brings to you in a mate. Also, pinpoint what you don't want.

Once you finish your list, ask God to help you with it. Where does it need rewriting? Where does your appetite need adjusting? Ask God if there's anything you desire that is off. Also, show it to a trusted mentor or two and ask them if the list is reasonable or superficial, and allow them to hold you accountable if Mr. Wrong shows up. I once had a friend tell me she had to have a man with a strong jaw line. If you have something like that on your list, hit the delete key! Grab some correction fluid.

I will share with you the traits I am looking for, as well as what I'm not. I share these vulnerable examples to show you what I consider important and to perhaps give you a starting point for yourself. Some are preferences; some are qualities I believe God would want me to wait for. Just because I'm publishing my list doesn't mean it's one hundred percent accurate of what I'm going to get.

CHERYL'S LIST:
THE KIND OF GUY WHO
WILL ATTRACT CHERYL

1. *A man who's strong in the Lord, has a sincere commitment to Christ, and loves God first above everything else, who can be a spiritual head of the household.*
2. *A man open to the Holy Spirit, prophecy, and who won't think I'm crazy because I believe God still speaks today.*
3. *A man who has a sincere heart toward me, and who will love me unconditionally as I am – and yet inspire me to be a better person.*
4. *A man who's responsible.*
5. *A man who's attractive to me.*
6. *A man who will make a great father and wants to be one.*
7. *A man who's affectionate, loving, and kind.*
8. *A man who is a good communicator – both listening and speaking – and is curious enough to ask me questions to find out who I am.*
9. *A man who will make family a priority, second only to God.*
10. *A man with a sense of humor, a playful kid at heart*

CHERYL'S HIT LIST:
THE KIND OF GUY WHO
WON'T ATTRACT CHERYL

1. One with unhealthy addictions (for example smoking, excessive drinking, pornography, gambling).
2. One who doesn't have control over his anger during conflict.
3. One who <u>currently</u> does not want to follow God's plan for sex within marriage only.
4. One who's antisocial, uninterested in being involved in my life outside the home or interacting with my friends or family.
5. One who has little interest in hygiene.
6. One who's lazy and not interested in working hard, lacks ambition.
7. One who doesn't believe that Hollywood or television and film is a legitimate missions field that needs Christians, one who doesn't support God's call for me as a writer.
8. One whose normal demeanor is excessively pessimistic.
9. One who's egotistical and thinks mostly of himself.
10. One who cheats, lies, or rationalizes dishonesty.

I occasionally ask God if He's up for a suggestion or two—especially if I meet a cool guy. Usually, God's answer is, "I'm not taking nominations." Apparently, because He's God, He does not need my help. (Imagine that!) I don't think there's anything wrong with making requests known to God. I also think we need to be open to Him changing our desires. I welcome that because I genuinely don't want to desire something or someone God doesn't want for me. I'm not saying I've written perfect lists or that even within these points I've listed that I won't have to find places to compromise. I know I can't compromise on the man's commitment to God, his desire to hear God's voice, and his openness to the Holy Spirit. I know women who are with men who are believers but still feel "unequally yoked" because they do not have the same beliefs about God. I want this important part of my life to be in sync with the person I am to spend the rest of my life with. I can't imagine this wouldn't be God's heart.

Trust God to lead you and protect you. If you ask God to write your love story, let Him write it. Be open to whoever He may ask you to be open to, including a guy who doesn't completely match your list. Just make sure the compromises you make are ones God is truly asking you to make and that it's not just your impatience kicking in. Especially be wary as your age creeps up. You may be tempted to say "yes" to the wrong person because you don't want to wait any longer.

Stop Daydreaming (aka Fantasizing) About Your Story

Is it acceptable if I just daydream about the man I hope God brings me? I once wrote a character named Nicole in my script @*Malibu High*—she had an active fantasy life. Every night before she'd go to bed, she'd imagine the life she wished she had. She'd enjoy cute little fantasies of all the ways her best friend, David, would declare his love for her. It was a cute device for a film script; I enjoyed writing her little fantasies. Each day back at high school, her reality would never live up to her dreams. Throughout the story, she grew disillusioned. She found that her favorite part of the day became those thirty minutes before she fell asleep when she could feel like she had the life she wanted. This was written as a teenage fantasy. Maybe it's cute at that age, but it's harmful, as an adult, to always imagine life being in a way that has nothing to do with reality. This is especially because, so often, fantasizing involves people we have crushes on who are not God's chosen for us. We feel emotional connections when we allow ourselves to ponder such scenarios. It feeds deepening feelings for the person. I encourage you not to allow yourself to do this.

Some of us may still be single because we are holding out for a perfection that doesn't exist. There may not be a guy out there who can live up to our standards, that "list," or the fantasies we allow ourselves to ponder. Just like I get sick of being told I'm not married yet because I'm still in preparation, guys get sick of feeling like they're not good enough to live up to a fantasy.

> *Cheryl's Journal (07/13/05)*
> *"I just finished* The Ultimate Gift's *final draft. I feel it's time now for the Gift of Love to come into my life. I can't wait to see what You're going to do with my life next. I have entered a new chapter. Lord, are You planning to surprise me tonight?"*

The Ultimate Gift

God is an amazing writer. I declare this with confidence because I've watched the writing He has done in the non-love-story part of my life. He's allowed me to live in many stories, playing important roles. In these, He's proven what a dynamite writer He is. Today, I can't give personal testimony of the love story God is writing for me. I want to share a time when God wrote a beautiful story for me to live in, testifying to the incredible role God's pen has played in my life.

In 2003, when God reminded me of the promise that I would one day get married, He also made another promise: He would open a huge door for me in my profession. He told me I would get a job writing a movie based on a book, and the job would come from Charlotte, North Carolina. There was even a description of the book: it would have a dark chocolate cover with embossed lettering. The person prophetically praying over me said she felt God would bless me with this job when I was in Charlotte on a free trip.

It just so happened that about six months later, I had a trip planned to Charlotte and had already ordered my ticket with frequent flier miles. So, I wondered what was going to happen on that trip. Would I somehow land a job writing a movie? It sure sounded like it. There was one piece of information that stood out. She said a chapel would mean something to me during that trip. I used to live in Charlotte; I never spent time in chapels there.

In November 2003, a book showed up on my doorstep, mailed to me from Charlotte, North Carolina, by a producer I had worked with on some books and audio dramas I co-wrote with Frank Peretti. The book was titled *The Ultimate Gift,* written by Jim Stovall. Its dark chocolate cover had raised lettering. The producer enclosed a note, saying he wanted me to pitch for the job of adapting this book into a movie. Naturally, I recognized that this was likely the project God was referring to; the pieces fit. The book arrived in time for my "free trip" — I'd be going to Charlotte in a month and would have a meeting with the producer.

However, this book came during one of the darkest seasons of my life. I was still extraordinarily depressed from the end of the relationship I thought was heading toward marriage. Writing was the last thing I felt like doing. I didn't have creativity and inspiration in me. To be honest, writing that pitch was tough. Around the deadline, the production company asked for my submission to put me in the running with the other writers. I turned in a work that I didn't like; I had to. I felt like God wanted me to have this job because of the prophetic words, but in my dry state, I almost didn't even want it.

I went to Charlotte for Christmas. I met with the producer, and he said they liked some things about my work but weren't ready to hire a writer yet. I left town — and that free trip — without the prophetically promised scriptwriting job. Also, I didn't spend any time in a chapel.

The experience was disillusioning. I couldn't figure out what happened. I thought maybe God talked about this blessing, but I had blown it by being such an emotional mess. January 2004 ended up being the darkest month of my life. After that time, I just let it go. I assumed something messed it up — me! The next nine months were filled with trials and challenges. God seemed to be working on me overtime. It was incredibly hard, and yet, also necessary.

In September 2004, I received a call no daughter wants to hear: my father was in the hospital having heart problems. He had just turned sixty years old—too young for this. The doctors insisted he have open-heart surgery, a quintuple bypass operation. My schedule was unusually clear. In fact, I was in need of employment. So when my parents offered to fly me home on one of their free tickets, I immediately jumped on a plane to Charlotte.

The producer of *The Ultimate Gift* found out I was in town through a prayer request email I sent out to my address book about my dad's surgery. He asked me to come in for a meeting. I almost didn't go because I wanted to spend every moment with my dad, but I felt like I should at least try. In fact, I prayed on my way to the meeting: "Lord, are You trying to bless me, and I'm being resistant?"

The time for blessing had come, even though I thought the job was gone because of my lack of creativity nine months earlier. That day, I walked out of that office with the job to write the movie version of *The Ultimate Gift*. It was a God-ordained gift that was such a surprise. God's timing was perfect.

On my drive back from the meeting, the fulfillment to all the prophecies hit me like a flood. I ran through all of them in my mind: the job writing a movie, coming out of Charlotte, the book description, the free trip, and this time:

The chapel.

My mother and I spent time praying for my father in the hospital chapel during his surgery. Suddenly, it was all clear. There hadn't been a mistake last December. I assumed something was going to happen before the right time. The time had come, and God showed up in mighty ways to give me His promised blessing.

I couldn't have written this story the way God did. I was living it. The inspiration followed because the right time had come. I had a completely different perspective on the story. I was now inspired to write it. The hospital chapel scene between two of the lead characters, Jason and Emily, was inspired by my time in that chapel.

When I reread the book, I noticed something remarkable. During the time God made me wait to get the job, He took me through many of the lessons the character in the book went through. In fact, He dragged me — sometimes kicking and screaming — through eleven of the twelve gifts outlined in that story.

One of the dominant themes of the book is "The Gift of a Day" and how precious life is. Having just walked through the possible death of my father one month before getting this job changed me as a human being. Never before had that gift meant so much to me as it did during the end of that free trip to Charlotte.

Now, here's where it gets ironic. God took me through eleven of the twelve gifts, to grow me up in Him, but what about the twelfth gift? It was "The Gift of Love" — the gift I clearly had been asking God to give me for so long. I playfully moaned, "God, You forgot one! You gave me all the trials, but You forgot the guy ends up with the gift of love. So get busy!" God didn't need my reminder, but I gave it to Him anyway. I know God appreciates my persistence! Ever heard of the parable of the persistent widow? See Luke 18.

There was one trial I added to the lead character's life that wasn't in the original book. One day, without any warning, all of his possessions are taken away. Just two weeks after I turned in the script with that additional story, I lost almost everything I owned because of toxic mold. When I noticed the parallel between my life and Jason's, I looked up at the sky and said, "Lord, could we not have chosen a different trial for Jason to go through?"

One of the most difficult parts of that trial was that I went through it predominantly alone. I had no guy in my life. I had to do most of the heavy lifting by myself, the moving, throwing everything away, finding a new home. It was a nightmare — for a season of time. It's one thing to lose furniture and clothes. It's another to lose journals, personally written stories, photos, scrapbooks, and other keepsakes. I had to get rid of every piece of paper or porous object.

As much of a nightmare as it was at the time, I always knew God was with me. I knew He was watching the situation. I knew He cared.

The fact that He had me write about such a trial, just weeks earlier, was an odd source of comfort. I also appreciated the order God chose for my crises. I would have given up everything I owned for my father to live. God had already carried me through that trial and helped my father recover. So, could I be upset when, just a few months later, He allowed me to lose almost all my possessions?

I wanted to share this story with you because it shows how intimately involved God is. He let me know this scriptwriting job was coming. He left out many details, but that's life. I got to live the story with Him holding my hand through every unpredictable scene and plot twist! I had no idea, when He first made the promise to me about the job, that the chapel reference would have anything to do with my father needing open-heart surgery. I will say, once I realized what it meant, it was comforting. It showed me how much God cares about details. It's like He has my life planned out, if only I'll follow the script He puts before me. Sometimes I go off-script and my freewill gets in His way.

I find that when He allows me to go through pain, I am able to use it in my writing to help other people. I hope you find ways to use what you've been through for others as well. You don't have to be a writer to use it!

A year after getting the job to pen the script, I got to visit the set for two weeks while *The Ultimate Gift* was filming. I even got to cast my parents in a hospital scene as extras. It was a poignant moment for me, being able to watch my dad see one of my biggest dreams come true.

God is an amazing writer, especially when we just let Him write — when we don't wrestle Him to the ground trying to get our pens back.

When I live through moments and blessings like this and see the payoffs of prophetic words, it helps me trust that God knows what He's doing with my love story. I spent a season in disillusionment, wondering what happened to this promised writing job. God still brought it to me at the right time. So, why do I struggle with believing God will deliver on the promise of a husband and a family? Those promises came to me the same day as the promise of the job that turned out to be *The Ultimate Gift.*

Do you have any stories like this from your life? Do you have times when you know God wrote an amazing story just for you? Obviously, it doesn't have to be tied to the love story area of your life. If you're reading this book, you're probably still waiting like I am for that story to break wide open. (For the six o'clock news, opening story!)

Our love stories are not the only stories God writes for us. Can you think of when God wrote just the right story in your work life? How about your family life? Have things happened to you that only God could have orchestrated? Has God found ways to use the drama, conflict, and challenges of your life, much like characters in a movie go through?

Embrace God's writing hand. While you're waiting for Him to write one area of your life, pay attention to other areas and try to discern what He's writing. Use this to build your faith. Write them down in journals. Write out His setups and payoffs, His themes and story crafting. Pinpointing the way God crafted the professional writing side of my life has built my faith that He's at work in the love story side, too.

As you may have guessed—despite the journal entry I shared about how maybe it was time for the Gift of Love to show up—it wasn't. Just a few days later, I journaled that out:

> *Cheryl's Journal (07/16/05)*
> *I have that creeping "ick" feeling that wonders if You're not about to change my life, like I thought. I have my own ideas about timing and how it should coincide with finishing this project. I need to know if my "now" hopes are erroneous and in vain. Please, Lord. Help me not be disappointed like always. I've weathered this journey for so long. Today, it happens to be weighing on me. Thank You for hearing my cry.*

Obviously, God's writing differs vastly from mine. In Psalm 23:1 (kjv), David declares, "The Lord is my Shepherd, I shall not want." If there's an area in your life where you are "in want," you need to submit it to God and allow Him to be the shepherd of it. We shouldn't want more than God Himself. I wish that were easier, though.

The sick person wants to be well. Singles want to be married. The childless want to be parents. Some parents wish they were childless. Some married couples want to be single. The hungry want meals. It's how we handle those aches that matter. Do we submit them to God? Do we grow bitter and blame Him?

God won't give us what we want if it will become a spiritual stumbling block to us. I believe God wants to give us our desires that line up with His will even more than we want them, but He won't until He can trust us to keep Him first. After all, He is the star of our stories, not us. He doesn't want to create a wedge between us.

Cheryl's Journal (04/02/06)

Father, I know you are watching over me. I want to be in Your will for my love life. Keep writing. Perhaps You've demanded a rewrite because there's one character out there who won't play out his role the way You desire. That's okay. I'm willing to pick up a new script, read new lines, embrace new plot twists. I'm yours. Write the script, and I'll play the role. Put me with a man whose life purpose can be fulfilled through me and vice versa. Put me with one who will follow You where You want him to go, and choose me for the journey. Lead and guide me always. Help me see, know, and discern Your will. Guide me rightly with a spirit of truth. Not deception. Walk with me through all of this and keep holding my hand. Don't let go.

CHAPTER FOUR
I Must Be Defective

FAVORITE REASONS I'M STILL SINGLE:
(According to others)

1. *God must think I'm not ready or mature enough for marriage.*
2. *If I didn't want to be married, then maybe God could bless me with a husband.*
3. *I refuse to sign up for online dating sites. (If you wonder why, see reason #4.)*
4. *I refuse to go out with anyone who isn't known well by people I know and trust.*
5. *I never call anyone who leaves a note on my car at Target that reads, "If you are single, I'd love to get to know you better." (If you wonder why, reread reason #4.)*
6. *My spiritual standards are too high. If a guy believes in Jesus, that should be enough.*
7. *I'm not trying hard enough to make something happen.*
8. *I'm way too independent. (The fact that I have no choice but to take care of myself seems irrelevant!)*
9. *I say no to blind dates with men twenty years older than me.*
10. *I don't always pluck my eyebrows.*

WHY I AM STILL SINGLE:
(According to lies I tell myself)

1. *I am not worth the trouble because of my imperfections.*
2. *I am not lovable.*
3. *I am not pretty enough.*
4. *A guy has to be drunk to be attracted to me.*
5. *I'm too old, even for guys my age, who want women ten years younger.*
6. *Another woman will always be there to take a guy's attention off me.*

Before we delve into this all-important, yet touchy chapter, I have a message for you:

There is nothing wrong with you!

Again, I repeat:

There is nothing wrong with you!

Did you hear me? Keep reading that sentence until you believe me. Sometimes, I need to hear it, too. We are about to walk through some of the most common insecurities we face — those of us who have been single much longer than we ever wanted to be. It's painful! There are many thoughts and emotions tied to this issue.

Now that we've established that, let's have some fun! Or let's find a way to laugh at the situations in which we find ourselves when facing other people's opinions or our own views about our marital status.

I found out the real reason I'm not married yet:

I am not blonde.

How did I figure this out? I conducted an experiment on the social networking site, Myspace. I created a fake page for an equally fake young woman. I named her Blonde Babe. My friend Caroline and I cracked ourselves up as we came up with Blonde Babe's life philosophies, interests, and favorites. Her favorite musicians were Milli Vanilli, N'Sync, and Menudo. Her favorite TV shows included *Baywatch* and *Xena: The Warrior Princess*. Her top movies, naturally, were *Legally Blonde, Clueless,* and *Dumb & Dumber*. Her favorite book was *Online Dating for Dummies*. The "About Me" section said: "I would love to post a photo of me and my blonde self, so you boys could see what I look like. I can't figure out how this Myspace thingy works. Maybe one of you fine young men can help me." (Insert blonde eyelashes batting here.) As soon as I finished the site, that's when it happened.

I received my first marriage proposal.

His name was Wally. He wanted me to move to Nebraska to live happily ever after with him, his buckteeth, and horn-rimmed glasses.

I thought, *Wow. All I had to be — after many years of waiting — was blonde, and a guy would propose.* Another guy wrote saying, "You sound like a fun gal! Let's get to know each other."

I'm not that naïve. Wally was likely no more real than my Blonde Babe was. Guys who'd be attracted to that profile don't interest me in the least. It made me laugh, *and* it made me think.

For any of my blonde readers: I mean no disrespect. I know we have different challenges to face, based on what we look like because of stereotypes people assign to us. I have incredibly intelligent blonde friends who are mistaken for ditzy blondes and treated poorly by guys. I have friends with perky breasts who can't get older men at church to stop giving them unsolicited backrubs. It feels just as lousy to be desired *only* for your physical qualities as it does to be rejected for them. It means men's pursuits have nothing to do with *who* we are.

Have you ever wondered if you're still single because of what you look like? If so, you are not alone.

Which Way Did My Self-Esteem Go?

I'm guessing if you are anything like me, your self-esteem has been battered by the question, "Why aren't you married yet?" It hurts— whether you ask or someone else does. I remember one couple that hounded me every time they saw me with the question: "Cheryl, when are you going to get married?" I'd snap, "I don't know. Take it up with God and get back to me because I'd like to know, too!"

It's hard to remain in this "not chosen" state and not have our self-esteems take hits. It's natural, but it's not reality. Our marital status is not an indicator of our worth or lovability, even though it feels like it is sometimes. That's a lie Satan would love for us to believe!

Have you ever tried to change who you are for a guy? Have you ever done something because you thought it would attract a particular person—like dyed your hair the guy's favorite color? It's easy to slip into this, rather than wait for the right person to love you for who you are. (In my case, dark brown hair and all!)

Psalm 139 is one of my favorite chapters of the Bible. It expresses in such a deep way how well God knows us, how meticulous He was in our creation:

> "For you created my inmost being; you knit me together in my mother's womb. I praise you because I am fearfully and wonderfully made; your works are wonderful, I know that full well. My frame was not hidden from you when I was made in the secret place, when I was woven together in the depths of the earth." (Psalm 139:13–15)

We may not be one hundred percent happy with the way God crafted us, but the point is He did! He chose our race, our frame, our family, our birthplace, birthday, and circumstances. He chose our eye color— and yes, even our hair color. He chose if we'd have the metabolism to be a thin runway model or not. While our lifestyle and health choices impact these issues, much of it was God's choice. Yet, often we resent

His choices. We think He made a mistake when certain guys want petite model blondes and we are tall, big-boned redheads. God doesn't make mistakes; He has crafted us perfectly for the place and time in which He chose our existence.

Considering our bodies are temples of the Holy Spirit (1 Corinthians 6:19), a gift from God, we need to be good stewards. We probably can do better when it comes to taking care of ourselves physically, emotionally, and spiritually. Just don't look at your appearance as the reason you are single. Well, unless you purposely don't take care of yourself. If you don't, you should consider adjusting your habits to reflect that you are one of God's princesses! More on that shortly.

Embrace who you are in Christ, including how the Lord made you look. Trust that God will bring someone to you who sees you as the beauty you are, the same beauty God sees.

Were you one of those young women who felt overlooked by guys in high school because of your physique? Did you have a best friend or sibling who couldn't fend off guys quickly enough?

My high school years did not include dates; I was not one to turn heads. (In eighth grade, I had the worst, curly haired perm imaginable!) While I craved male attention, I also watched the multiple heartbreaks of girls who were prettier, more desirable to guys. I saw how destructive dating in high school could be. Because I wasn't caught up in relationships, I focused on my dreams and goals for my life. I spent most of high school writing and acting in plays. I joined theatrical troupes. Can you see what God was setting up? God knew He called me to be a writer. High school began this all-important training for me. If I'd used up those years dating, what would I have to show for it? A few more heartbreaks. Instead, God used that time to train me for His purposes for my life.

Have you had stretches of time where dating or serious relationships were nonexistent? Did you spend the whole time fretting about what you didn't have—or did something fruitful come out of it?

What did God do with those seasons? How did He prepare you for your life's purpose? Did He give you a way to serve and help other people? Remember to look for the gems to come from seasons like that.

Modern Day Esthers

Speaking of you all being God's princesses, I would be remiss if I didn't mention we should try to do the best to be "ready" physically. Even Esther went through a year of beautifying treatments before she could be presented to the king. She wasn't changing who she was. She was enhancing the gifts she already had.

During some of my driest dating years, I have to admit I didn't try to attract men. I did not keep up with styles. I wore clothes that were two sizes too big, trying to hide my body and what little shape I had. I still had an eighties hairstyle when we were more than halfway through the nineties. All of that has changed now. While it doesn't seem to be helping me get dates at the moment, I have more confidence. Perhaps one day, the extra effort will pay off. (Incidentally, I do pluck my eyebrows now.)

Are you taking advantage of your best traits? While we don't want men to only care about what we look like, since they are visual creatures, we should try to look our best. In the same way, we probably would like them to look their best for us. We don't need to do this because we're defective; we're taking advantage of the gifts God's given us. Hopefully, we can do this in a way that is tasteful and doesn't cause the men in our lives to stumble.

How Ready Am I, Really?

There was a time in my life when a person could have said to me, "You are not ready for marriage" and it would have been true. In this fallen world, many of us have issues we need to face. I was one of those people. So, even though I poke fun at the sentiment, sometimes there are legitimate reasons that we might not be ready to get married yet. I had to get emotionally healthy, so once I do get married I can enter that marriage whole, not dragged down by baggage.

Is there anything from your past that you feel you should heal from before you start a marriage? Marriage should be about two healthy people entering a relationship because of love and God's will, not because they need fixing or are seeking something from marriage that only God can give or restore. This could involve healing over past relationships, hurts, physical or sexual abuse, family issues, challenges with a father figure, unhealthy addictions or habits. Ask yourself if there is anything you need to deal with now that would benefit your marriage later. Work on those issues first.

I spent many years in and out of counseling, reading self-help books about my issues, and engaging in healing prayer ministries. They worked! God showed up and did a mighty work in me, but it took a while. I'm so glad God did the work before marriage and independent of a man. I used to think God would use the love of my life to heal me; I was wrong. God wanted to complete that work Himself first. He was the potter; I was the unwitting clay.

When God finished this healing work in me, I wrote my autobiography, *Finally Fearless*. It deals with my past battles with a panic disorder, mainly tied to my fear of men and intimacy. Because so many of my issues were tied to relationships, I'm waiting to pen the final chapter of that book—*Chapter Twelve*—until I get married.

"Chapter Twelve" has become my nickname for my future husband. Usually I say, "God, where is my missing Chapter Twelve?" Remember the story where I prayed to God about the missing "Gift of Love"? It's the twelfth gift in *The Ultimate Gift*.

Cheryl's Journal (12/03/07)

Is stuff on hold in my life because of something I lack? If so, what, Lord? How perfect do I have to be to have love in my life and a husband? It's hard for me to imagine being my age, with my birthday in a week, and I'm still not "good" enough or ready enough. There are many "less ready" people who are married. Why do I feel I have to arrive at this unobtainable place of perfection before this can happen? I guess in my life, I just don't see others having to be so perfect to find love. It's hard for me to believe I'm not judged "worthy" of love yet.

Is Perfection the Key that Unlocks Love?

Is God waiting for us to reach perfection before He'll bless us with a husband? I wondered about God's competence at the marriage prep table if He couldn't manage to get me ready after all this time. Then I questioned His judgment. If my future mate and I are not together yet because of my husband's preparation taking this long, then why did God choose that person? Why not choose someone who would be ready close to when I was? I felt like God told me in 2004 I was finally healed and ready. Why tell me that and then still not deliver? I was trying to reason this out and understand God — who, incidentally, has no interest in being understood. Just read the Book of Job!

I found out, through a heartbreaking situation, that God is not waiting for me to be perfect. I've mentioned God made a promise to me through prophecy that I would one day get married. He also promised I'd have a family. A friend I knew back East, much younger than me, also had received the same prophetic promises of marriage and a family. There was one big difference between her and me:

I wanted this gift; she didn't.

I figured since she was young, perhaps with time she would desire these gifts the Lord had for her. She wasn't aching for these promises to come to pass; it didn't matter to her if they ever happened.

But they did.

Within a short time of us receiving our identical promises from the Lord, this young woman met a Christian man and fell in love. They got married. Soon after, they had a couple of children. Just like the Lord promised!

I battled feelings of jealousy. I wondered what was so wrong with me that God considered her ready and not me, even though I was so much older. I didn't understand. Why give someone a blessing they don't want, when the one who craves it stands by alone?

A couple years later, I got a "wake up call." This young woman chose to end her marriage. Again, I found myself asking hard questions about God and His ways. This taught me that we shouldn't make assumptions about what God is up to. I thought God blessed her because He considered her ready. Obviously, the situation wasn't what I thought. I imagine the freewill of human beings got in the way of God's plan, and I bet God's heart must have ached.

I believe when God makes us wait, it's often about timing. Yet, God can continue to work in us to prepare us for the best chance at having successful marriages. The odds stack high against marriages lasting; we need all the help God offers. Let's drop the belief that we are not good enough—that if no one's chosen to love us yet, we're not worthy. My so-called striving toward perfected readiness hasn't brought the gift, but my flaws haven't kept love away, either.

If You'd Just Make Jesus Your Boyfriend…

Sometimes, we say the stupidest things, don't we? People often pointed out one of my major, so-called flaws: I desired marriage. Apparently, the key is to not want it. (God must find humor in the ways we think we're helping one another!) It reminds me of Job's friends who gave him bad advice as they tried—to no avail—to explain God. It's true, some of us can be so obsessed with the desire to be married that it forces God to wait until marriage is not an idol. How often, when a friend has a new boyfriend, does that friend stop spending time with the rest of her buddies and focus solely on the guy? Well, until the break up, of course!

Is it valid to think that if I don't want marriage, I can have it? Well, I'm the first to say I've tried; I've tried hard. I've prayed countless prayers to God saying, "Please take this desire away." But He hasn't! I even asked, "Just take the desire away until you're ready to give it to me. Hold it in a box. Duct tape it closed for later because I don't want to desire anything that you don't have for me right now! It hurts too much." Well, He hasn't granted that request either, but surprisingly, He did tell me why.

I felt God say He would not dull this ache, this desire to be loved, chosen, and treasured by someone. Why? My ache over one person not choosing me yet gives me understanding for how God feels. He aches over every person who doesn't love, choose, and treasure Him. Lest we think God doesn't understand how we feel, He has to face this same pain exponentially more than we do. I felt like He asked me if it would be appropriate for Him to dull His own pain over those who reject Him, just so He wouldn't have to feel the pain. Naturally, that didn't make sense. Of course, He feels it! He chooses to allow me to feel the same pain over the one who's "missing."

God also made it clear that the pain He allows fuels my calling, my writing. I couldn't write this book from a place of understanding if God had dulled my pain. I couldn't write scripts and books that touch hearts if I didn't feel the way my characters feel. He's chosen this for me on purpose. I just have to decide if I will let Him use me in my pain or grow bitter that He hasn't given me my husband, yet.

When God called Jesus to do His will, that calling was extraordinarily painful. So, I should not be surprised God's call for me also includes pain. Instead, I should be honored that He's willing to use me, a broken vessel, to help others, even if it means being lonely much longer than I ever imagined or would have willfully chosen. Sometimes, I moan, "Seriously, God! Did You have to choose me as the poster child for the single-and-waiting-on-God girl?"

Are you willing to ask God why He's chosen this path for you? Are you open to letting Him use you in it?

Admitting You Feel Pain is Not a Defect

Are you honest with God about how you feel? It's meant so much to me when God has shown up with an answer or an illustration, showing His understanding of me. There are also times I cry out in journals and feel silence in response. The following entry is one of those times. Warning: I sound like a moan-head, filled with self-pity. I'd rather show you my raw, honest journal entries than pretend I always have the best attitude and the most surrendered heart. We've all had these moments. (Right? Please tell me I'm not the only one who occasionally indulges in self-pity.)

> *Cheryl's Journal (2006)*
>
> *Why is this such a hard promise to fulfill? What is the big deal? Why is it so much easier for everyone else to find love? Some who didn't even have to ache for it. I guess since I have zero control over this, all I can do is beg God to move. He is the One who asked for the pen of control over my love story. He has it; I don't. I've done nothing to try to create a situation. I've sat and waited but still been open, watchful. So, Father God, please write. How do You want me to position myself while waiting? I already told You to keep whoever this man is until he's ready. Why can't You get him to cooperate with You? You are the most powerful God ever, the supreme being of this universe. Can't You get just ONE GUY to love me? You know this is the position I have been in my entire life. Unloved. Unknown. Not chosen. Can't You write the line that says this guy finally wants to spend time with me?*

From that journal entry, the story that has become *Never the Bride* was born! I decided to take my pain—and moaning—and turn it into a comedy. The story centers on Jessie, a girl who accuses God of being asleep on the job of writing her love story. God shows up to face the charges. He tells her He can't write her love story unless she's willing to surrender the pen. It's the purple pen she's held onto her whole life, journaling about how her love life should go. None of her fantasies match reality! There's a funny scene when she makes up her mind: she wants to give God a chance and surrender that purple pen to Him, but

God is nowhere to be found. So she breaks into a church to drop it off at the altar. Of course, she gets caught. (And hilarity ensues!) I figured my pain should at least come in handy to help others, right? Even in the form of a comedy.

The Universal Pain: Rejection

Years ago, I had what I call the year of rejections. I would find myself interested in godly men, but no one ever looked at me the same. Then, a particular guy entered my life and wanted to spend time with me. I loved our spiritual compatibilities. My interest in him was solely based on his godly qualities. As I began to hope our friendship could move toward something more, his communication abruptly stopped. Weeks later I endured one of *those* conversations. You know, where the guy sits you down at the local Starbucks and tells you he stopped talking to you because he just started dating someone. Your close friendship is no longer appropriate. Again, I felt overlooked for someone else. Though, I must recognize he did exactly the right thing. God bless him for making a choice and going after it and drawing new boundaries with his female friends! I took a prayer walk after, asking God why this keeps happening to me. Crying out my frustration over the entire year, I said, "God, why don't you just hang a sign on my head that reads 'never the choice'?" I said it in anger. Suddenly, listening to the sound of my self-pitying voice, I started laughing. I glared up at the sky and said, "That's going in a script, isn't it? That line. This moment." Indeed, it did end up in *Never the Bride*'s script.

After each rejection, I've weathered moments of doubt where I wonder, *Am I crazy? Why do I believe God is writing me a love story? Am I waiting for nothing?* Usually, I come back to a place of faith, a place where I believe wholeheartedly God is taking good care of this for me. Most of His work is behind the scenes, out of view. God doesn't often take me into His story meetings to let me know what He's up to.

I want us to see rejection as a gift from God, not Satan's attack against our lovability. God allows rejections from the wrong guys. He doesn't want us with them, especially not if we've asked God to write our love stories. I often ask God to blind every man to me who isn't the right guy. Then I find myself offended when no one ever likes me! I feel overlooked, undesirable. (Sounds like God can't win with me, doesn't it?) I don't want the wrong man showing me attention, so I won't be tempted to go the wrong direction if he is not God's chosen.

Have you ever been thankful for a rejection after the fact? Maybe a month or a year later? The rejection may have hurt at the time, but it's often easy to see later why it's good we didn't get what we asked for. (Ever heard Garth Brooks' song, *Sometimes I Thank God for Unanswered Prayers*? It should be our theme song.)

REJECTED IN GOOD COMPANY:
(Where to find kindred spirits in the Word of God)

1. **Leah**—Jacob loved Rachel but was tricked by her father into marrying the older, apparently less desirable sister, Leah. Jacob was not quiet about his displeasure with her. She's even referred to as "the one who wasn't loved." (Genesis 29–30.) It's heartbreaking to read her many attempts to win over Jacob's love.

2. **Joseph**—He was thrown in a cave and sold into slavery by his brothers, then separated from his family for almost two decades. (Genesis 37.)

3. **Ishmael**—Can you imagine being the *un*promised child? (Genesis 16.) Then, once the promised child shows up, you get sent away. (Genesis 21.) Even if God heard him crying, the boy still had to feel a monumental amount of rejection once Isaac arrived. I'm sure his mother, Hagar, also felt bad about herself.

4. **Moses** — He battled feelings of inferiority as a speaker and a leader. (Exodus 4:10-13.) Everyone would complain to him daily about his leadership skills, their unhappiness, the lack of tasty food, blaming him for the mess they were in. (Numbers 11, Deuteronomy 1.)

5. **David** — First he's "chosen" out of all his brothers to be the new king. Then King Saul goes from enjoying David's soothing harp music to throwing spears at him. David lived on the run for years because of Saul's hatred. (1 Samuel 16–31.) Check out Psalm 22 if you want to see David crying out from a place of rejection. ("But I am a worm and not a man, scorned by everyone, despised by the people." Psalm 22:6.)

6. **Isaiah, Jeremiah, Ezekiel, and many other prophets** — Their messages from God were adamantly rejected, as they never told people what they wanted to hear. They endured ridicule because of their faithfulness to spread God's messages.

7. **Hosea** — How many times did his wife cheat on him, even after he accepted her back? Hosea 1 recounts how God told him to marry an adulterous wife. In Hosea 3, God tells Hosea to show love to his wife again, even though she was with someone else.

8. **Paul** — How many times was Paul rejected for sharing Christ's Gospel? How many times did he endure trials, persecution, flogging, stoning, and imprisonment? He embraced all of this rejection and considered it all worth it for the cause of Christ. Paul had a way of understanding life isn't about the here and now, the pain we experience now. Philippians 3:13 reminds us to forget what's behind and keep our eyes focused on what is ahead of us.

9. **God** — It's heartbreaking to read the Old Testament and see how often God felt grieved by the Israelites, His chosen people. His words express the extreme amount of pain He felt each time they chose idol worship over Him. He sounds like a scorned lover. His prophets often used lover terminology when they described the Israelite's unfaithfulness to Him. The phrase "forgotten the LORD their God" is in the Bible several times.

10. **Jesus** — Our Savior experienced the harshest rejection of anyone on earth. Not only was He ridiculed, flogged, beaten brutally by commoners and lawmakers, He was rejected, denied, and abandoned by His disciples and friends. He was turned over to authorities by a friend who became a traitor. Then, on the cross, He had to experience the ultimate rejection: the moment where He cried out to His own Father, "My God, my God, why have you forsaken me?" (Matthew 27:46b.) He came to save the world, yet few believed Him.

When I recently told a woman the story of my character in *Never the Bride*, she said, "Surely, it's your choice to be single!" In a nice way, she figured if guys had anything to say about it, I would not still be available! I told her flat out it was not my choice.

I have to face that my singleness right now is God's choice, not mine. It's not because I'm defective. It's not because I'm unlovable, unworthy, not pretty or blonde enough. It's because for whatever reason, *God has decided it's not time yet.* I can use this time wisely, for the Lord, doing what He needs me to do. I can improve myself in natural ways where I honestly need it. I can combat lies I've been fed — internally, by the enemy, or by others. I can choose to stand on who I am in Christ, and trust that when the time comes, God will deliver on this promise of the gift of love.

I hope you will believe the same for yourself. Even if we are not defective, there are still ways we can grow through God's training. In the next chapter, we'll train through Marriage Boot Camp together.

Cheryl's Journal (09/28/03)

Cheryl's prayer: Lord, why am I still waiting? Where are these promises?

God's reply: Trust me. I have your best interests at heart. I will not leave you empty. I take your heart, restore it, and give it back. It's yours to offer with sincerity and grace. Be ready. Keep your eyes open. Keep watch. Stand on My promises. It is not a question of your lovability. It is My thwarting to not allow love to begin until it's the one that will last. The one who will love you the way I want you to be loved, and treasure you the way I want you to be treasured. Do you want a gift before it's wrapped? Before it's paid for?

CHAPTER FIVE

Marriage Boot Camp: How Loving God is Similar to Loving a Husband

---

WAYS CHERYL IMAGINES A HUSBAND MIGHT GET ANNOYING:

1. *He'll fall asleep long before me — because I take forever — and then I'll be stuck awake because he'll snore loudly.*
2. *He'll hog the covers; I won't be able to pry them out from under him, and I'll freeze.*
3. *He'll put his dirty feet on me; yes, I still happen to dislike feet.*
4. *He'll try to come into the bathroom when I am in much need of some privacy. (There are certain moments we don't need to share.)*
5. *His presence means I'm going to have to do laundry more than twice a month.*
6. *He won't feel like putting everything back where it belongs, even though there is a place for everything.*
7. *He'll buy big objects that we don't need or can't afford.*
8. *He won't want to eat what I feel like cooking.*
9. *He will ignore me when his mind is on another track.*
10. *He'll choose to have a distracting crisis just when I'm on a creative writing high.*

I have a question.

How am I supposed to keep a healthy relationship with the One who has the power and ability to "fix" my life—which, in my opinion, means to give me a husband—and yet, He still won't do it? How can He stand by and watch my pain of loneliness and still refuse to move? How should I feel about Him?

Welcome to Marriage Boot Camp—God style—where your spiritual muscles will be stretched, built, and sometimes overworked beyond the legal limit. There are many parallels between a relationship with a husband on earth and our love relationship with God.

Rather than seeing this time when God leaves us stranded—oops, I mean single—as a waste of time, we should use this season to practice principles vital to successful, godly marriages under God's guidance. If this helps us be better wives later, we have everything to gain. The fact that God is working on us should bring hope. God wouldn't waste His time on us if we weren't worth the effort. We are worth every moment of His time. In case you haven't heard, marriage can be difficult. Take this intimate season with God—when He has you to Himself—and don't waste a moment of it! Because when it's over, it's over. I feel certain I will miss it.

Okay, so, did my pep talk work? Are you excited? Motivated? I can understand if the subject matter of this chapter gets under your skin. It references us needing to love God, even if He's not cooperating with us. Please remember: you are *not* defective! Being in a prep season doesn't mean you are.

To make it through this time with our relationships with God in tact requires a specific type of love:

Unconditional love. Welcome to the first Boot Camp Principle—the most challenging of them all.

Boot Camp Principle One: Love Unconditionally.

How often do we hear our married girlfriends complain that they need something from their husbands and they won't budge? Obviously, the same goes in reverse. Many wives don't give their husbands what they need either, but let's not get distracted by that at the moment. God asks me to love Him unconditionally, even when He doesn't do or say what I want or what I think I need.

Being in a love relationship with God is great practice for being in a relationship with a spouse. That's why it can feel a bit like conditioning; we're in training for "battles" ahead. Spouses often won't do something the way we want them to and especially not in the timeline we want. If we can learn to accept this part of God first, how much more adaptable will we be in marriage?

I'll share a journal entry that came to me after a heartfelt prayer about the delay in my marital relationship. I felt like God spoke to me about how He wants me to love Him and how He feels about my prayers:

Cheryl's Journal (05/12/05)

God: I want you to love Me and to love Me first, far and above this love story I am telling you. Come to Me and sit at My feet and petition Me about something new. Something fresh. Trust Me with the rest. I have heard your cries. I know your cries, your hopes and dreams. I know how much you want this to begin. I've heard every one of your prayers. This is not all our relationship is about. I've been trying to restore you. To clean you out, to melt away all that needed to be shed. To rid you of the dross and all that was weighing you down. You are My impatient daughter. I have done much to work in your life and a quiet day makes you restless. This is the first of your quiet days. Take the rest. Embrace it. It's My gift to you. Sit at My feet, instead of working. Rest in My presence. Let Me heal you and your heart. You will not settle back into the life you had. I want you to change. I've ordered this change. Do not resist Me and the work that I am doing. Let Me do it. I am not through with you yet. No, My work is never done.

Can you sense God's heart to be loved for who He is and not what He can do for us? Let's look at the biblical view of love. The Bible has a lot to say about marriage and the relationship between a husband and a wife. I encourage you to read, study, and meditate on the following passages: Ephesians 5:22–33, Colossians 3:18–19, and 1 Peter 3:1–7. 1 Corinthians 13, known as "The Love Chapter," is wonderful to meditate on what love really is.

What is love? Is it flowers, gifts, and chocolates? (Mmm. Especially dark chocolate.) Is it a romantic date? A thoughtful present? A kiss? Sex? You won't find any of those words in 1 Corinthians 13. Instead, you'll find such words as patience, kindness, not being easily angered or keeping a record of everything a person does wrong. It also includes not being boastful or prideful or envious or self-seeking. What do these have to do with love? This is how God says to love one another. (Not that God isn't romantic and doesn't delve into the occasional love story. Peek at Song of Solomon!) Take the time to study what God says about love and marriage in His Word, and be awakened to how much it doesn't talk about romance. Sometimes, when we're sad about not being married and wallow in our loneliness, it's romance we crave. A person to kiss or snuggle with. A hand to hold. But that's not all that love is. Love gives us the chance to be long-suffering with someone, or the chance to put another's needs far above our own.

Most of God's words about marriage imply women need love and men need respect. It's simple, but it isn't easy. We can get our practice now with God.

Boot Camp Principle Two: Love is Not Based on Feelings.

Sometimes, we feel excited about our love for God; other times, we feel a bit stale, dispassionate. For example, you know how in the first three months of a relationship, you're in that "honeymoon" stage? Everything feels exciting. You can't wait to see the person. After that opening season, the excitement dies down. Those flutters in your stomach halt. The "honeymoon's over" as they say. (Whoever "they" are. Not me because I've never been on one. Oh, but I will! Don't worry! It's on my undated calendar and several to-do lists.) A similar thing can happen with God. Remember the first moment you became a believer or that time you went through a revival? You couldn't get enough of God, the Bible, church services, fellowship groups, or prayer. The excitement dies down eventually. It comes back at various points of the relationship. Just like in marriage, there are ebbs and flows in the passion.

With God, we learn how to manage these ebbs and flows, and we try to keep ourselves on track with God even when the excitement dies down. Our relationship is not supposed to be based on emotions and feelings; it's about commitment. The same is true of marriage. Being able to remain faithful in relationship with God in the midst of those less exciting times is great practice for marriage.

Boot Camp Principle Three: God, Then Our Future Husbands, Need to be Top Priority.

God needs the number one spot. Our husbands will be second. That's still high up there. God is a jealous God and isn't going to put up with idols—those other priorities we make more important than Him. Learning to prioritize God first is good practice for learning to make our husbands our first *earthly* priority, second only to God.

God knows what I need better than I do. If I put Him first, He will take care of the rest. When He closes the door on a relationship I want, I should be on my knees kissing His feet, not yelling at Him for not giving me what I asked for. Keeping Him first and not letting this desire become too important is good practice in prioritizing.

Make a list of your priorities, everything that takes up time in your life. Evaluate where God is in the midst of it. Is He the most important priority? Is work? Is your desire to be married or whatever you are doing to search for that M.I.A. dude? What is your relationship with God about? Are your prayer times focused on the needs of others and your spiritual growth, or are most of your prayers geared toward what you want God to do for you?

Boot Camp Principle Four: We Must Have Great, Two-Way Communication.

God wants us to have time for talking *and* listening. Our prayer lives are the lifeline of our relationship with God. It isn't just about us talking. Rather, it's a dialogue: two-way communication. Obviously, marriage needs the same. While I love God for His patience with my voluminous prayers, I know it's far more important that I hear what He has to say. He already knows what I'm thinking anyway! I'll admit, sometimes a silly rant is therapeutic. I apologize after and sense God smiling and shaking His head at me.

To follow is an example. I'll share a heartfelt prayer followed by how God responded:

> *Cheryl's Journal (2005)*
>
> *This ongoing rejection is excruciating. You say You want to take care of this for me, but You keep letting me get hurt over and over. I started this new journal with hope in my heart, and again, it seems it's shattered. Lord, I've cried out to You for so long with my raw pain. You know my whole life has been characterized by never being loved, chosen, or treasured. This scenario You've written for me has put me right there. It's the same place I always find myself: unloved, not treasured, and not chosen. Why is that? Is all of this worth the pain You keep me in?*

After I prayed this, I suddenly felt God's presence. I was in bed and felt this sensation moving across my forehead, almost like I had a thorn sticking in it. I felt a dull pain. Next, it felt like drops of blood were dripping down the sides of my temples, as if from the thorn. I had to resist the urge to reach out and grab my forehead because I knew if I did, it would stop. I knew something spiritual was taking place, not physical. I remained motionless for five minutes, as this sensation continued.

I emailed a prayer mentor about the experience. She said it reminded her of Philippians 3:10a, kjv. "That I may know him, and the power of His resurrection, and the fellowship of His sufferings...." When I told two other prayer mentors, they also gave me the same verse to help explain what God was doing in response to my tearful prayer.

If anyone understands rejection, it's Jesus. He, through the cross, experienced the harshest rejection of anyone on this earth. Jesus was letting me know He understood my most recent pain of rejection. Even though God hadn't spared me from rejection, I appreciated that He showed up to let me know He was paying attention. I felt His deep love for me that day. This is why two-way communication is so important. What God had to say to me through this unique experience was far more important than my words. I also love how He showed His love for me even in my anger. I questioned His character and His loyalty to me, and yet, He poured out His love in return.

Boot Camp Principle Five: Anger Must Be Dealt With Swiftly.

In our relationships with God, we will experience anger and disillusionment. We can practice making peace with God, even when He doesn't do what we want Him to do. Let's just accept that He will make us angry. He will—in our opinion—not always do what's best for us. It is what's best, but God's definition will contradict ours often! Remember in Isaiah 55:8, God reminds us, "'For my thoughts are not your thoughts, neither are your ways my ways,' declares the LORD."

We have to face our anger with God honestly, just like we would need to face it with a spouse. God can take our honesty. We also need to make amends. Ephesians 4:26, which advises us not to go to bed angry, applies to God as well as a spouse. There will be days we won't feel like talking to God, yet we need to. We need to be honest with Him. We shouldn't give God the silent treatment. Do I need to clarify it probably won't produce great results from our husbands either?

Are you willing to ask God to help you grow in your reactions to situations that frustrate you? If you have a problem with your temper or expressing your anger in a non-loving way, don't be embarrassed to ask for help. Seek counsel and the prayers of your mentors.

Boot Camp Principle Six: Let God Be Himself.

Have you ever dated anyone who wanted to change you? Aggravating, isn't it? Let's not frustrate God by trying to change Him or change the way He does things. It's a wasted effort anyway, since God has a mind of His own. He's sovereign. The idea of not trying to change someone is easily translatable to a husband, isn't it? Practice letting God be Himself. Then you'll be well prepared to let the man you marry be himself.

Boot Camp Principle Seven: Wait on God.

While we wait, we need to practice trusting that God has a reason to make us wait. Most of my future wife muscles have been built and strengthened through God's fire of waiting. Once I get married, waiting on God is not going to stop. My future husband and I are going to weather waiting together: waiting for direction, for answers, for jobs, or when God chooses it's time to start our family. (Hey God! I'm thirty-something right now, in case you forgot. That impacts my family, doesn't it?) The waiting fire will always be part of our lives. I've dedicated an entire chapter to this topic!

Boot Camp Principle Eight: Be a Servant.

Be ready to serve God in whatever area He asks. He has assignments for all of us, daily, weekly, and long-term. Those assignments change.

Our future husbands will become a part of our God-ordained assignments. My married friends tell me marriage is about serving the other person. It's not about what we get from our spouses. Selfishness needs to be wiped out. This is tough; we are selfish by nature. Jesus is our best example of a servant throughout the New Testament. Ephesians 6:7 reminds us to serve as if serving God and not men.

Boot Camp Principle Nine: Learn to Trust and Have Faith in the One You Love.

Just like a husband, one of the most important things to God is trust. He treasures our belief in Him, our belief that He is who He says He is, that He'll do what His Word tells us He'll do, and that He's trustworthy. Nothing motivates a husband more than knowing his wife trusts him implicitly. Our husbands won't always do tasks in the time or way we'd like to see them done. They want to know we trust them to do what we need. God wants the same trust, no matter what means He uses to give us what we need. We often hear what's most important to a man is respect. Trusting God—and eventually your husband—shows you respect God and His judgment.

Boot Camp Principle Ten: Be Faithful, Loyal, and Committed.

Faithfulness, loyalty, and being committed are three of the most important values we can embrace. We live in a world where cheating on spouses is rampant. I've heard too many stories about people who thought they would never be vulnerable to cheating feeling tempted. Have we ever stopped to think about the ways we can be unfaithful to God? He is never unfaithful to us. Yet, how easy is it to find other priorities or walk away from Him during a rough patch?

Do you know people who've left the faith when God didn't live up to their expectations? It happens in marriages, too. You hear them say, "This isn't what I signed up for. This isn't what I thought it would be." People who feel this way may choose to cheat or leave their spouses and break their vows. I've often been concerned about my own tendency to romanticize marriage and underestimate how hard it can be. Choosing to be faithful no matter how hard it gets is vital to marriage. Starting now — remaining faithful to God regardless of what He allows to happen in our lives — is invaluable practice.

Cheryl's Journal (05/11/05)

> *Cheryl's prayer: Lord, why are you so hard to understand?*
> *God's reply: I am uncontainable. I don't want to be understood. I want to be loved. I want to be cherished. I want you to be My bride that loves Me unconditionally no matter what I do. No matter what I say. No matter what I do not say. Even when I do not speak. Love Me. Don't try to understand Me. We are communicating, even when I am silent. I am speaking volumes to you when I am silent. Don't resent those moments. There is much to be learned in that time. Accept it as all part of the package of loving Me and being My bride. I will be silent often. Yes, it helps you see the difference of when I speak and when I close My mouth. Always remember, no matter how silent I am, I am never gone. I am with you, even if I am not saying a word. I let you speak as much as you feel the need. I enjoy spending time in your presence, even when you are angry with Me. Even when your words are unfavorable. I know it's all part of the fire I am sending you through. I accept this. I can take it. I want that close communion with you. We have a real relationship.*

I hope you are encouraged to know that if you are stretching in any of the areas discussed in this chapter, it's time well spent at the weight bench. I don't mean to come off like an expert on marriage: I'm not! I've just been in God's Marriage Boot Camp way longer than I ever thought I would be, with God making sure my muscles don't atrophy during the wait. I appreciate the revelation that God has shown me: every way in which He stretches me while I'm single is to my benefit later — and yours, too. So hang in there with me, and bench press! You can do it!

CHAPTER SIX

If My Maker is My Husband, How Come He Never Takes Out the Trash?

WANTED:

- *A man who can open jars*
- *A man who won't mind walking me to my door at night*
- *A man who will drive me to the airport so I can finally stop using dangerous shuttles (or a bus that takes three hours)*
- *A man who can drive me places, since I hate driving and parking (especially down dark alleys alone)*
- *A man to share adventures with, who will invite me into his world outside the box I've been in for so long*
- *A man to go to events with, so I never have to walk into a place alone again*
- *A man to share a meal with*
- *A man worth learning to cook for*
- *A man to kiss and hold hands with*
- *A man to write romantic songs for me*
- *A man who likes to sit on a porch swing and talk the night away*
- *A man willing to ask questions and dig deep into who I am*

> *Message for My Man:*
> *If you don't show up soon, I'm adding you to the FBI's Ten*
> *Most Wanted List. It won't be pretty! I will not bail you out*
> *of your first night of captivity.*

Apparently, my Maker is my Husband. That's what Isaiah tells me in chapter 54. Actually, that chapter talks about Israel. It also discusses God's compassion, His promises, the barren woman, and how His love can't be shaken. It's a beautiful chapter, one of my favorites.

How does it translate into our lives? If God wants me to make Him my sole husband, in what ways is He truly a husband to me? In what ways is He not exactly like one? Since I always like to the look on the bright side of life, let's first recognize the awesome ways God is a great Husband to us, surpassing what we'll find in an earthly husband. (I mean no offense to my future husband; I'll still like you, too, even if God is cooler.)

God is a Great Listener
God usually doesn't get tired of my stories, my endless repetition. If He does, He doesn't let me know! I go through old journals and see how often I prayed the exact same prayers, using the same phrases. I annoy myself, yet God is patient. He hears my cries, and He listens more than He talks.

God Speaks to Me
Whether it's through His Word, through another person, through a sunset or a purple flower, through a God Wink, a dream, a vision, God speaks. He directs, guides, lovingly corrects, and encourages me when I need it.

God Designed Me for a Purpose

God is the only Being in this world who knows fully why He created me. Therefore, He directs my life. Husbands cannot give us purpose. God may choose marriage for part of our ministry. Our future husbands are not mapping out the course of our lives; instead, they are mates designed to join us on the path God has for us (and vice versa). The Bible has a lot to say about purpose, God's will, and paths for us. I suggest you do a word study on those concepts, and seek the Lord about what He wants you to do with your life.

God Saves My Tears

God is the only One who knows all of our deepest pains. He pays attention; He puts our tears in a bottle (Psalm 56:8). No one else can match this attention and care for our hearts and emotions. A husband is not going to know every time you cry; God does. He pays attention.

God Reads My Mind

We don't need to tell God what we're thinking. He already knows, yet we can tell Him anyway because He listens. Can you imagine what it would be like to have a man who can discern what you're thinking? How many marital fights are caused by one spouse not knowing what the other is thinking or feeling, even when they're communicating? With God, this isn't a problem. Men are constantly frustrated by women who assume they can read their minds; God does this naturally.

God Can Be Everywhere at Once

How many times do women complain that men don't show up when they need them to? We don't have this problem with God. We do have His invisibility to deal with, but regardless, God goes with us everywhere we go. He never misses an appointment.

God is Always on Time

I'll resist snide remarks on this one—about God's sense of timing. This statement is true, regardless of how it feels sometimes. He knows the day, the hour, the minute that something in particular needs to happen in our lives. He may not be early, but He's never late.

God Puts My Best Interests First

God sent His Son to die for us. He gives us the gift of salvation if we choose to receive it. Like most caring parents, God does what's best for us, even if we can't see it. When a parent doesn't do what a child wants, that child doesn't always believe that the parent has a good reason. We occasionally treat God the same way. God gives us exactly what we need, even if it doesn't always feel like it. There are times He will allow painful situations into our lives. He can use them to fulfill His purposes, or sometimes they're just part of life or an attack of the enemy. Regardless, if we want our lives to line up with His will, we need to submit to His process.

God is the Provider

We may think we need a husband to provide for us financially. We don't. God is the source of blessings. This includes work and incomes. I know God has provided for me in wonderful, miraculous ways throughout my whole adult life. Let's not forget the man comes with a second set of expenses, and maybe even different spending habits than you have.

The Ultimate Gift is one example of God's provision for me. That job came through at the perfect time. God chose that work for me and opened the door. He does the same for us whether we are married or not. He's the One who lines up our assignments. Even if you ultimately get a husband who has a good-paying job, who do you think gave that job to your husband? God. We need to stop looking to the guy as if he's the one taking care of us. Once married, we don't want to pressure him as though he is the only source; God is the Source. Of course, they are the ones who go out and do the hard work just like we do. We just have to remember the One who provided those jobs in the first place.

Those are some of the qualities we could only wish to find in a spouse. We won't find the same degree of them in an earthly husband! They may have their moments showing some of those good qualities, but God is the One who is consistent. He surpasses all men! Only God possesses that kind of greatness.

WHY IT'S BAD TO BE SINGLE:
(An itemized list of undisputable evidence)

1. Outside my parents and my sister and her family, I have no family or children of my own.
2. I have no immediate support system to come home to, when life throws its challenges and curveballs.
3. I'm lonely.
4. I have no one to go to parties or special events with. When big events happen – even when they're good – I walk in alone.
5. I never get to take advantage of the "two people can combine resources and live together cheaper than apart" deal.
6. No one loves me. (My mother's love doesn't count in this case. Sorry, Mom!)
7. There's this constant question about many guys I meet: is he the one? Is he worth dating? The search feels never-ending.

8. *There's the continuing heartbreak of liking guys who have no interest in me. (This happens a lot!)*
9. *I can be selfish sometimes because there isn't that person to care for daily, whose needs are above my own (spouse or children).*
10. *There isn't anyone to cuddle with, enjoy affections with, sleep beside (or let's be honest — have sex with).*

This is not meant to be discouraging. If anything, I'm including this chapter to say to you, "I get it!" Do your well-meaning friends and family tell you that God as a Husband should always be enough for you — the same ones who probably have spouses? Technically, they're right; God is enough. Does it always feel that way? No. We are human. God created us for companionship. I get tired of feeling condemned when every day of my life I can't honestly say, "God as my Husband feels like He is enough." Again, I didn't say He *isn't* enough. I'm saying He doesn't always *feel* like enough. Please see the difference.

I want to use the rest of this chapter to admit why we sometimes feel this way so, at the very least, you know someone out there understands how you feel.

You'll notice in each section, I am going to offer counterbalances. Where it may seem God falls short in the "natural," He makes up for it in the spiritual realm. This isn't because He has anything to make up for! It's because, on a spiritual level, what God does for us is so much greater than any man could do in the natural. Let's take a look at both sides.

The Heavy Lifting

Though I've heard stories of God supplying extra human strength, often we feel helpless to do what our muscles can't do. We feel like we can't do stuff on our own, but no one is there to help. I lost count of how many weeks my extra futon mattress sat in the middle of my living room floor because I couldn't find a guy available to help me throw it out. Nothing makes me cry quicker than when I can't do something on my own and no one is around to lend a strong hand.

Cheryl's Journal (04/07/05)

Why is it okay with You that I have to do so much alone? The physical labor alone during this unexpected move was ridiculous. Why is this okay? Is this best for Your daughter? I don't understand why You continue to not give me my life partner, the one who can ride these ups and downs with me. Why promise changes to me, yet continue to send trials? God, I know You don't owe me anything, least of all an explanation. But I don't get You! I know by Your Word that You love me more than anyone could. Why does Your version of love hurt so much?

That journal entry refers to my move because of toxic mold. It involved much physical labor. I couldn't understand God's choice to keep me alone for yet another huge trial, but He did. Ultimately, I came to appreciate that special time of transition that moved me from my old life to the new. For the first time ever, I got a chance to live alone. I got a place where I have an office, a separate area to write. It was an amazing difference from where I was living, where my bedroom was my office and I spent most of my time there. (Side note: I thought God was giving me a year tops to live alone before I'd get married. That was 2005. I was wrong. Though, I still enjoy living alone.)

I do want to say when it comes to lifting heavy emotional burdens, God wins, hands down! His Word reminds us of this: "Take my yoke upon you and learn from me, for I am gentle and humble in heart, and you will find rest for your souls. For my yoke is easy and my burden is light." (Matthew 11:29-30.) His Word also says, "Cast all your anxiety on him because he cares for you." (1 Peter 5:7.)

Where's My Housework Helper?

Sometimes, I put praise and worship music on while I clean house so I can feel like God is with me, but He doesn't grab a dust rag and start wiping off my 32" LCD. Each time my VCR eats a tape (yes, I still have one), He doesn't grab the Phillips head out of the messy tool drawer to take it apart.

However, I want to share a story about when God was being a Husband, even though, at the time, the situation felt abundantly frustrating.

I was away on a writing trip. While I was gone, my apartment was getting new piping. I knew I'd have some cleaning up to do upon my return. When an opportunity opened for me to leave the writing trip on a flight that would get me home ten hours earlier than scheduled, I jumped at it. It would get me back at three o'clock in the afternoon instead of one o'clock in the morning. I had no idea how important those ten hours were going to be until I arrived.

I walked into a house filled with soot. Not only had the plumbers almost burned down my apartment, they broke down drywall without covering anything. So, there was a layer of dust on top of every piece of furniture, my bed, my books, my toothbrush. My bathroom sink was stopped up and my toilet was endlessly running. I almost flipped out. I happened to make it home before the plumbers left for the day, so I could get them to fix my bathroom clog. I had to wash every piece of clothing, vacuum every surface. Oh, and clean up all the mud they tracked in over my rug and kitchen floor.

For about the first six hours of cleaning (with three hours worth of jet lag), I was so angry — angry I had to clean up this disaster by myself. As the day wore on, in my angered moments, I kept saying, "Thank God I got home ten hours early." I would have arrived at one a.m. with no ability to spend the night. One a.m. to me would have been four a.m. with the time difference. By that night, after eleven hours of cleaning, I told God that while I was upset I had to clean up by myself, I was abundantly thankful that in His way, He had been a true

Husband to me. He got me home early enough to do the work before I went to sleep that night.

If you find yourself in a situation where you're upset because you don't have a husband, try to keep your eyes open to the ways God gives you that extra dose of grace to deal with that situation.

Who's Walking Me to My Car Late at Night?

While God may not walk us to our cars in the visible sense, I strongly believe He does protect us with His invisible angels. I've had my most vulnerable moments as a single person late at night going to my car. I hate it.

I've had many guys *not* ask me if I wanted to be walked to my car. I've found myself too ticked to ask. I figured if anyone tried anything, I'd smack the person over the head. However, let's admit it: married women have this problem, too, as they are not with their husbands 24-7. I erroneously internalize it as though it's a problem exclusive to singles.

One night, my car was having mechanical issues. I had to drive straight to my mechanic's shop, leave the car, and walk the rest of the way home. So, that's what I did. Did I mention it was about 11:15 p.m.? Not my brightest moment. I prayed the whole way that, if there were anything unsafe about it, God would protect me.

That night, I woke up from a nightmare with this haunting thought about how God was not writing my love story. I felt I'd been kidding myself. It's those vulnerable moments that can set off Satan's attack.

The next morning, God felt like a Husband again. My car was ready by 8:00 a.m. and my mechanic said the problem was so simple he wasn't going to charge me. I felt taken care of that day, even though I still woke up alone.

When you are concerned about walking alone late at night or if you find yourself in a situation where you feel vulnerable, I encourage you to memorize verses from Psalm 91, a great chapter about God's protection. Quote the verse, "For he will command his angels concerning you to guard you in all your ways." (Psalm 91:11.) I've heard many stories about people being protected while alone when a perpetrator thought they saw another human being with them. In reality, it was probably an angel.

Where's Mr. Fix-It Guy?

In general, when items break around my apartment, I can't do much about it. I heard once that guys like to come to the rescue when a girl asks. So when my vacuum cleaner broke, I put out a call to a guy. "Would you mind taking a look at my vacuum cleaner? I can't get it to work." Apparently, he didn't want to come to my rescue because he didn't even want to try. He quipped, "I don't know anything about fixing vacuums." So much for that! I took the stupid thing apart myself and fixed it. It's a good thing I figured out how; that was the first of about sixty times I've had to perform the same surgery on that vacuum cleaner. Perhaps God showed up with wisdom, and I was unaware of it. Usually in my household, if it breaks, I throw it out.

To put this in perspective, I'd like to point out that while God may not always swoop down to fix broken material possessions, He shows up to fix our broken hearts and spirits when we need it. He can put the pieces of a life back together like no other, forming a beautiful mosaic out of the shattered glass. That's way more important than any object that falls apart. Remember: God is near us when we are brokenhearted (Psalm 34:18).

Where is my Nurse?

I had to have surgery on my foot, which I knew was going to make me dependent on other people for at least two months of no driving. Before the surgery, I was fearful about going through it as a single person. I wasn't sure I'd have enough help, since my family lives 3,000 miles away. I even said to a friend, "Remind me next time I have surgery to be married." I figured that would mean someone is obligated to take care of me and this process wouldn't be so difficult to endure "alone." To prepare, I stocked up on every supply I could think of, cooked two months worth of food in advance and froze it all, and I did everything else I could do to prepare. I still needed help. I needed rides to the doctors, people to shop for perishables for me, people to wash my hair, or even just to keep me company. There were chores that God wouldn't specifically do for me. He sure provided wonderful friends to stand in the gap. I never went without.

There was one afternoon, during the first week of surgery that my helper had to cancel. I couldn't figure out how I was going to feed myself. I used my crutches to move over to the fridge, to see if there were anything I could reach without falling over. I could not. I thought I would have to skip lunch that day. Right then, a neighbor knocked on my door, carrying a warm, home-cooked meal. Talk about amazing, God-ordained timing!

Honestly, it didn't matter that I had no husband to take care of me. It showed me that, even when certain situations seem like they can accent our singleness, God is there with the grace to help us endure. It also reminds me as a single to keep my eyes open to the needs of other singles in situations where they need extra help through a difficult time.

God, Do You Realize, as My Date You are Invisible?

Yes, God can escort us anywhere we go, but His invisibility does not work in our favor when He takes His single brides out on dates. When I am feeling down about my singleness, nothing will convince me that walking alone into a party—with God—is any match for showing up with a date. Not when you suddenly have to face your ex! You know— the ex who drapes his arm around that blonde he found after you.

I've had many prayer mentors tell me to go to these parties knowing the Holy Spirit resides within me and to feel confident. Sometimes, it works. Other times—like when my surrendered attitude to the single season is *not* in check—it doesn't work. It feels crappy to run into an ex when you're alone. I'm not saying how I feel is right. In fact, it's probably a bit on the wrong side, but I promised to be honest with you. So, there!

> *Cheryl's Journal (12/10/06)*
>
> *Lord, You know I've been frustrated, angry, and tired of being in this same old, dry-bones place. It's painful to sit here, on my birthday, and see life hasn't changed. I'm still alone. A particular hope was dangled in front of me, and I was tricked into thinking I'd finally have a date for my birthday. My extreme disappointment and pain isn't this guy's fault. I can't go to that party unless you plan to surprise me with a date. I'm in the same fight Jessie has in* Never the Bride. *The invisible date is just not enough. Lord, I need healing. I need You to fix this. I need You to move.*

Sorry you had to read that, but it's how I felt at the time.

Have you ever noticed how the devil can take a blessing and try to turn it into something ugly that hurts you?

One day, I got the good news: *The Ultimate Gift* won a Movieguide Award as one of Top 10 Family Films, plus two other nominations. Sounds like great news, right? I should have been excited about the red carpet, black-tie affair in Beverly Hills at the same hotel where they hold the Golden Globes. After all, they were honoring my work. I was excited...

Until they asked me for my guest's name.

That's when anxiety came over me. *Each ticket is $1000 and they're offering me one freebie. For a date. Who is that supposed to be? I don't have a boyfriend.* There was someone in my life I was interested in, but I didn't know if he was right for me. I didn't want to invite him if he wasn't. It just had too much potential to send my brain down the "he's your missing ultimate gift of love" track. I had no chance of getting a "real date" for an important event. I had plenty of guy friends ask me to take them. That's all they were: friends. I didn't want to share this event with "just-a-friend."

I cried out to God: "Why do I have all these amazing things that happen to me—and yet I have no one to share them with?" Notice how quickly I lost sight that the nominations for three awards was a blessing.

I prayed, "God, the awards show is just two days before Valentines Day. If I were writing my story—which clearly I'm not because I wouldn't write this delay into the script—you can bet I'd send Cheryl her final and true love in time for this event. It would be followed by a special Valentines Day dinner later that week."

It's amazing how quickly Satan can use what's supposed to be a blessing and a gift from God to derail you into a place where you're thankless for the gift. You focus on what you don't have instead.

My solution: I decided to borrow someone else's husband. (That's what we single people resort to sometimes.) Only in my case, the choice was an honor. I invited the director/co-writer of a movie I wanted to work on in the future. So, I turned it into a work deal. That was much better than the angst of bringing a non-date for no apparent reason beyond my lack of ability to get a real one.

Sometimes, we have to be smart in what we do with our loneliness. My solution worked, and I had a great time.

Incidentally, just when I finished processing the whole Movieguide Awards angst, I got another phone call. I was the winner of a CAMIE Award for *The Ultimate Gift*. The question came: "Would you like to bring a guest to the televised awards show?"

Can We Be Honest about God, Sex, and Fatherhood?

Those of us who are single have to deal with our frustrations about how engaging in sex shouldn't be part of our lives outside marriage. Plus, without being Jesus' mother Mary or taking a trip to the sperm bank, we are not going to get pregnant as celibate, Christian singles.

There are many people who won't wait. I've had times where I've pondered what I'm waiting for. Thankfully, I feel like God's given me grace to wait for His best. I believe God has designed sex exclusively for marriage on purpose and that it is the only right way. That's prevented me from giving in to sex outside marriage. I'll admit it's incredibly hard to just watch even simple affections between other couples—dating or married. The handholding. The kisses. The intimate dinners at restaurants. I feel like there's this whole world—especially with sex and intimacy—that has never been a part of my life. It's such a mystery to me. I have married friends who say, "You don't know what you're missing!" (No, duh!) There are others who say, "Oh, it's such a duty now!" They are not fans. It's perplexing. Regardless, it's a void, a void I've chosen to keep in my life until God blesses me with a husband.

Just because I've made the choice to wait for marriage to have sex doesn't mean that it isn't difficult. Believe me, it is!

There was a time I let a guy spend the night. Just a friend. We were sleeping next to each other. (Note to self: this is not a smart way to avoid temptation.) *Nothing* happened that night, but for three days, I was crushing on him. I can't imagine how other girls who sleep around deal with it. If my head gets messed up over just sleeping *next to* a guy, what would having sex do?

Later on, I let another friend stay over. We kissed. I kept thinking I should feel bad. I thought, *Wow! I must be so starved for affection that I feel I can justify this behavior.* I know it's probably not God's preference. He wants me to be content lying next to His invisible body, but that doesn't always feel good enough to me in my flawed, human state.

I confessed this to a married friend. She said her husband had been out of town for a week, and she was aching for him to be by her side at night. She lovingly said she doesn't know how I do it, having gone this long sleeping alone. She gave me grace, but this wasn't something I wanted to make a habit of. It brings complications into your life, especially when friendship lines get crossed and you have to figure out the next day if that meant anything.

Our bodies were made to be touched and to have sex. So these days when we wait so much longer—those of us who do try to wait—it's difficult. So, I caution you to be more careful than I've been.

Precursors to marital intimacies only tempt and frustrate. Though they might momentarily simulate marital closeness—even if it's actual sleeping and there's no foreplay or sex involved—these things tease your heart. They give you a false intimacy and can leave you feeling more alone, even devastated, in the morning.

I also want to encourage you that, if you have made the mistake of having sex with someone who isn't your husband, you can be forgiven. Receive the blanket of comfort that comes with forgiveness only God can bring. Then commit to not make the same mistake in the future.

I hope this section encourages you to see that wherever God may not be something to us in the natural, He sure makes up for it in the spiritual realm. In a later chapter, we'll explore the many benefits we have exclusively as singles. First, in the next chapter, we'll share some stories we can all relate to—some hazards of singlehood.

TO DO LIST:
Continued from Chapter Two
(Additional things Cheryl must do
before she can get married)

1. She must stop hating the following verse: "But let patience have her perfect work, that ye may be perfect and entire, wanting nothing." (James 1:4, kjv.)
2. Write this book super fast in case God decides she's getting her husband upon completion.
3. Forgive every guy who's ever rejected her and try to squeeze out a thank you to God for guiding them to do that.
4. Work out more. (After all, once she gets married, she's gotta get naked! Yikes!)

CHAPTER SEVEN

Tales from the 'Hood: Singlehood

THINGS THAT MAKE ME WANT TO PUT GOD ON PROBATION:

1. To God, "soon" could mean 2,000 years.
2. His promises often take a long time to pay off.
3. He doesn't care about my timetables and deadlines.
4. He doesn't take any of my suggestions.
5. It doesn't matter to Him that my birthday keeps changing my age.

I was eight years old when I caught my first bouquet at a wedding. That says it all about how that superstition works, doesn't it?

In this chapter, we're going to talk about everything in society that makes it tough on us as singles. Again, this isn't a free pass to indulge in self-pity. I want this to be an encouragement so you see that *you are not alone*! What we experience is felt everywhere. We may think everyone else has someone except us, but it's simply not true. So, come on. Buckle up! Let's laugh and cry together as we dig into our common areas of angst.

#1 Hazard of Singlehood: Holidays & Birthdays (Another Year Passes)

It's official. I'm going to declare a new holiday:

National Singles Day.

I'm not talking about National Singles-Awareness Day, which the rest of the world knows as Valentines Day. I'm talking about a new holiday. How about the third Saturday in June? Right smack in the middle of wedding season! Yeah, that's when it should be. That's the day, every year, when married friends need to shower their single friends with gifts.

It's abundantly unfair, the volume of weddings we get invited to either attend or be in, bridal showers, baby showers, anniversaries. They don't just hit our wallets; they can be a source of highlighting what's missing. Our friends and family members always have special occasions to receive gifts. We do all the spending or party-throwing. We go through the angst of having to find dates for all these weddings or risk feeling ridiculous at a table by ourselves, while all the couples dance the Macarena, the Hokey Pokey.

I find that holidays, special occasions, and family gatherings have a staggering effect on me at times when I'm feeling sad about my marital status.

If you're ever in a large group setting, it's also when the suggestions come out. "Why aren't you signed up for online dating?" "Do you want to meet my best friend's cousin?" "Have you considered it might be about your fashion sense (or the lack thereof)?" "Maybe if you'd pluck your eyebrows, you'd snag a man!" (Yes, someone said that to me.)

I'll share a few of my journal entries that all sound the same over the pain of each passing birthday:

> *Cheryl's Journal*
> *(11/20/05) I'm sad to know my birthday is coming and I can already tell that You haven't reserved this gift for me in time for*

my birthday. It's disappointing. I've hardly journaled over the past month. I guess it's because I've tried not to care about this.

(12/09/05) I dread the stroke of midnight. You know what my expectations were when I was this age. So much for that. My birthday is coming tomorrow, and I wish it weren't. It seems my hopes are so often dashed. They've never had the chance to be fulfilled. I'm sad to still be alone.

(12/05/06) I'm so sick of my life. The chapter I want doesn't get written. I'm always stuck in the "wait" chapter. Am I in the Act Two climax of Never the Bride, *so I can be shocked by whom God ushers in? The one I didn't see coming? That phrase "Never the Choice" rings in my brain.*

(12/10/07) This week, I didn't want words and promises. I wanted life to answer — life to unfold, rather than the picture of a future life yet still unobtainable. I didn't want the on-going promises and reminders. I wanted life to happen. Not just words.

One year, near my birthday, I felt a strong pull toward a particular person. My birthday didn't turn out like I'd hoped — he forgot my birthday. That night in prayer at a Bible study, someone gave me a word from God.

God said I'd made assumptions and jumped to erroneous conclusions. The illustration included a lighted path and how I had been stepping ahead of God's path. That should have been enough to tell me that particular guy wasn't on God's list. However, for months I still wondered, pondered, and asked, "Is it just not the right time?" God was saying "wrong person." I was rewriting that into "He's not who he needs to be yet."

Sometimes, I have no idea what I hope for and how what God has in mind is much better than I'd choose. Given that it was close to my birthday, I was more forgiving of traits I probably wouldn't want to live with in the long-term. I wanted the "single" status fixed by that birthday! Clearly, God didn't care about that because He spent my birthday reprimanding me for focusing on the wrong guy.

Honestly, it's not that the guys I liked were bad people. In fact, they'd probably make great husbands for other women. This is more about whether a particular guy is best for me in God's eyes and what He has in mind for my future.

#2 Hazard of Singlehood: Married Society is Clueless of Our Plight

Our society doesn't make it easy for the single person. There are things in life we have to deal with that married people do not. They include stigmas, people trying to fix us, to "solve our singleness," blind dates, a multitude of broken hearts, failed relationships, unrequited crushes, going to special events alone like high school reunions, family gatherings, holiday feasts.

So often, people look at the single woman as though she needs to be fixed—or that she apparently needs their help. They call on their second cousins to "take this woman out!" It can be humiliating.

Sometimes, those who are married forget what they felt like when they were single. They act like everyone in their world is married. This happens so often in church.

One Sunday, a woman got up in church to make an announcement. She said, "It's the event you've all been waiting for! Finally, a married couples' retreat." I mused about how there's truth to that. I *have* been waiting for years to go on a married couples retreat. However, I would not be invited to this one. It always bothers me when people from the pulpit forget their audience. Not everyone who goes to church is married! Many churches skip our demographic and offer us nothing. They go from the college and career group to the young marrieds. They forget that many these days are in their thirties and forties, yet alone. Mother's Day can also be a hot button for some women who desire children.

A friend went to a church where the speaker talked about Proverbs 31, which details what makes a good wife. The passage says that being a wife and mother is the noblest thing a woman can do. This pastor used that verse to suggest any woman who isn't married or a mother is not fulfilling God's perfect plan for her life. He supposed that if the Bible holds this position in such high regard, those who are not wives or mothers are not doing something God needs them to do to enter this place of nobility. Sermons like this can be painful for single women or childless couples.

I also find that society doesn't understand my choices about dating and what I'm doing (or not doing) about it. People harass me about not "making it happen." If I could make it happen, believe me! I would have by now!

I prayed for wisdom from God about how I don't have what others say is a healthy dating life. I'll share an excerpt from my journal of what I feel God said to me about this:

> *Cheryl's Journal (08/31/07)*
>
> *God: Think of the ark, methodically built, for such a time when no one understood what Noah was doing. There was no precedent for it, but he built it at My command. This is who you are. You are one who obeys even when no precedent has been set. Even when it defies logic or human tradition. You listen to Me about men. This pleases Me. Keep your ear tuned. Take these moments with Me. Know My character. Know My thoughts. Listen to them. I have many thoughts toward you — as our relationship is an intimate one, and will continue to be. I am your Husband. One and only Husband. I have a helper for you, but I will always remain your True Love. Your First Love. This is right and good and will be the foundation of your strong marriage. Your prayer closet will be the life of your marriage ministry. There will never be a time you won't cling tightly to*

Me. You will always consider Me. Your eyes will always search. Your mind will always wonder what I am up to. I love your curiosity. I love your honest seeking. I love our times of blessing, our prayer closet moments. This time alone is precious; this time is rare. It will come to a close once I invite someone into your life, someone you will share your life, time, prayers, body, and soul with. You will be a praying couple. You will be a ministry couple. My Spirit will flow actively through you both. You are both leaders for My Kingdom, My sheep, those who need to hear but don't. The priority you place on Me is needed and will grow. I am your life, your lifeline, your everything. Keep Me in that place. I am your refuge. I give you rest, creativity, ideas, anointing. I am your taproot. All you need is inside Me. Tap into Me and you will find it. I give life and blessings overflowing. Let Me give you words to help those who challenge you. Consult Me for answers. I have life-giving words to share through you. Let Me be your anchor. Let Me be what you hang onto, cling tightly to. I am yours and you are Mine, My love.

#3 Hazard of Singlehood: Dating

Blind dates. First dates. Setups. Mix and match. Let's talk about the hazards of dating. Personally, I hate dating; I've never been a fan. It's one of many reasons you won't find me surfing online date sites. I can't stand the idea of going out with someone—especially one I hardly know—trying to figure out if we're compatible enough to warrant a second date. How do you tell that person you are not interested in round two? How do you know he's not dating a bunch of other people once you decide you like him? There is nothing I like about the process. Some people enjoy it and just look at it as a chance to go out and have a good time, try on a bunch of different personalities and see what they like and don't like. Some look at it as a way to get free meals or movies. That doesn't work for me. I find it too awkward. I feel like it has the potential of bringing much pain into my life or into the life of that guy, if I don't end up feeling the same.

How often do people give you advice about whom you should date? One time, my family was in cahoots with this guy's family about getting us together. The guy was unaware of the set up. When I met him, I quickly determined we weren't compatible. We had nothing in common, even though he was a nice guy.

A mere eight months later, he found *and married* the love of his life. Thankfully, my judgment wasn't off that time, but it's awkward when others try to force their opinions on you about whom you should like. When you don't feel it's right, they think you're turning down an opportunity and prolonging your own singleness.

I want to be clear: I'm not saying it's wrong to date or online date. Sometimes, it's just what you have to do, or want to do. In my life, most of the time, I've become friends with guys first. That can have its hazards too. I'd like to know if I can handle being friends with a guy before adding all the trappings of romance to the equation. How quickly can hormones and kissing get in the way of good judgment?

#4 Hazard of Singlehood: What Makes a "Real Date" or a "Real Relationship"?

That brings me to another hazard of singlehood: when is a date a real date? When is a relationship a real relationship?

Let's start with the date. I have some friends who say an invitation for coffee alone with a guy constitutes a date. If that were true, I've dated a heck of a lot of men. (Trust me, I haven't!) Maybe there was an era where any invitation to go out with a guy alone was considered a date. Today, however, that isn't true. You can't even assume, if you're out for coffee or a meal with a guy and he chooses to pick up the tab, that he looks at the outing as a date.

It's so confusing these days. I had one guy friend from college take me out to dinner. I'd heard him argue the point strongly that any outing with a guy and a girl is a date. However, when I began to develop feelings for him and the topic eventually came up, his answer was: "I just don't think of you that way." It wasn't even that he dated me and decided he didn't like me. He never thought of our outings as dates. Maybe I was an exception. I don't know.

I spend a lot of time alone with guys. I have incredibly strong friendships with quite a few. If I were to define time spent alone as a date, then I've had lots of them. Even simultaneously.

I've gone out with guys, wondering, even hoping they saw them as dates, but not too far into conversations with them, I could tell they weren't. I don't think any of those guys in my life would say they've been on dates with me. (If they think otherwise, it would be news to me!)

I've resigned myself to the belief that until a guy says, "Would you like to go on a date with me?" I will assume every invitation is not a date. Some of this is self-preservation. The moment I hope a guy's invitation spells interest in me is about the time he tells me he wants to ask out one of my friends. Or, my personal favorite, the guy says he's decided to get back with his ex—the same ex I endured ninety conversations about after their breakup.

To help with this section, I took time to quiz some of my guy friends. It was fun hearing what they had to say about this. I asked each of them, "How is a girl supposed to know when an invitation from a guy is considered a date?"

One said an invitation is not a date unless a dating relationship has been talked about and established. He said a guy wants the right to invite a girl out to get to know her without having the pressure of defining if he's interested in her. Sometimes, he can't answer that until he spends time with her. Another guy said if a girl wants to know, she should ask the guy. Another guy said he spends a lot of time out with girls alone and hardly ever considers those dates. (No, he didn't know how the girls saw those outings!) Yet another guy pointed out that sometimes, outings are initiated by women—and we're the ones who start calling them dates after much time has been spent together. The variety of answers from these men proves this is not an exact science.

Now let's talk about the other side of this. When is a relationship a real relationship? Does that seem like an odd question or have you found yourself so close to a guy that it almost seems like you are in a relationship but it remains undeclared? Are neither of you dating anyone, so you are each other's "go to" person for events when you want to bring someone? When a crisis arises, is he the one you call (and vice versa)? Are you there for each other like a couple that is dating and yet you have no sense of security because nothing official has been established? Have physical boundaries not been crossed and feelings not been discussed?

This is what I call "The Best Friend Syndrome." So often, we fall for our best friends. We'd do anything for them, wouldn't we? I always said I wanted to marry my best friend. How come, so far, I haven't married any of them? I've left those friendships feeling like I was hung out to dry. These are usually the friendships where everyone in your life asks, "Are you guys dating? You seem so close." With your mouth, you say, "No, we're just friends." In your mind, you think, *How come everyone else but him can see that we're a great match?*

As women, we crave emotional intimacy and support. We are nurturing. We love to give this gift away to men we like, in hopes they'll see our incredible value, see how much we contribute to their lives so the friendship will grow beyond that state.

What's the problem with this? I don't know about you, but I rarely see these friendships move into anything else. The guy gets everything he needs—emotionally and practically—from you, while you are left hungry and aching for more. Most likely, the guy will remain content to let you serve him and be there for him the way you have been. The fact that it will never go further isn't bothering him. He gets what he needs from you; you get *some* of what you need from him. It's not likely that your hope for more will be fulfilled the way you want.

I put this warning in here because it's a mistake I have made time and again. I'd look at a friendship and think, *Wow! We have such an amazing foundation for a dynamite relationship once he's ready.* There's only one problem: the guys almost never see it that way. They'll never be ready. If they felt something for you, this type of friendship wouldn't last long in this state before transitioning to something more.

Not being so generous with our emotional support is something we must practice. It's not about playing games; it's about protecting ourselves. No one should gain that place in our hearts and lives until they make a move toward committing to us. It's too hard to contain our hearts and emotions when we get so close to men in these types of friendships. I heard one pastor call these "one flesh friendships." He borrowed the term from the Bible about becoming "one flesh" like spouses do, but for singles on an emotional level. We can easily become complicit in this problem, too, enabling guys to continue using our emotional availability to feed their continuing fear of commitment. Like with sex, if we give up too much emotional availability or intimacy without commitment, we're setting ourselves up to get burned.

A couple times, I've had to tell my "best guys" I couldn't be close friends with them anymore, or that we needed to recalibrate our relationship to the "just friends" label they had put on us. It's so hard; it takes much willpower to give up the emotional connection this person has offered. I feel like if a guy is not pursuing after a reasonable amount of time, he isn't going to. Playing that head game that says, "He just needs a little more time to see how wonderful I am" prolongs the inevitable—and that is the pain you are going to feel when you have to give him up. You'll lose him to someone else or because you decide you won't wait anymore for a newly defined relationship. And you know what? Remaining in that friendship makes you appear unavailable to other people. You may be delaying the start of the right relationship because the right guy thinks you are with that "best buddy" you seem to be with, even though you're not.

There is the adage that men and women can't be close friends. Either a relationship will begin, or one will have feelings and the other won't. As time goes by, I've come to believe this is almost always true.

Having to give up some of my favorite guy friends because of this has been one of the most painful parts of being single for me.

#5 Hazard of Singlehood: The Wrong Relationships

Our impatience can lead us to the wrong people. We are on our search; someone catches our eye. We hope it's "him." The right "him." Our desire for the search to be over can make us try to mold that person into who we believe God has for us. Often, we are wrong. If we don't wait for God's best, we may end up with the wrong person. We could derail God's plan for our lives.

Samson is one biblical example where a man ended up with the wrong woman. He chose Delilah. Samson was so captivated by her that he let himself be worn down by her endless prodding into what the secret of his strength was: his hair. God told him not to tell anyone that secret. He was too blinded by his love (and lust) for her to see through to the motive of her badgering.

When we read the story (Judges 16), Delilah doesn't seem the least bit subtle. She continuously asks for the secret. Every time Samson gives Delilah the wrong answer, people try to harm him in the way they believe will remove his strength. Why he continued to be with her and trust her is anybody's guess! Clearly, he was with the wrong woman.

When he broke down and told her the truth about his hair, she had it shaved and he lost his strength. The consequences to his life were huge. He was captured, had his eyes gouged out, and spent the rest of his life as a blind slave. Was it God's plan for him to do this? I believe Samson was living the consequences of being in the wrong relationship and disobeying what God told him.

There may be someone in our lives who appeals to us but is not God's choice. It's hard to resist those people, but if we do enter the wrong relationships, we can pay big consequences. God can still use us, no matter what choices we make. Wouldn't we rather make the right choice the first time, or allow God to make the right choice and be patient until He's ready to give him to us? I often say I'd rather be alone than with the wrong person, even if the wrong person feels right for a while. It's not worth getting in the way of, or delaying, God's true calling on my life.

#6 Hazard of Singlehood: The Heartbreaks

I don't want to take away from the fact that we learn and grow sometimes from the wrong relationships. Plus, some relationships are not wrong just because they don't lead to marriage. All past relationships are part of our journey to the right one. Some of these can still be God-ordained, even if they end in heartbreak. Others, we potentially chose for ourselves when we didn't feel like waiting on God. When they ended, we suffered the consequences.

One thing we singles have in common is that heartbreak is huge in our lives. This happens when we desire to date someone who has no interest in us or when we date someone and one of us decides the relationship isn't working. This is one hazard of singlehood I will gladly shed when I get married. Of course, marriages break up and, sadly, heartbreaks exist on that side of the fence, too. We just go through them more often while we're on this seemingly endless search for someone to marry.

#7 Hazard of Singlehood: The Wrong People Interested in Us

How hard is it to wait for love when someone shows an interest, but you're sure he's not the right guy? Then you have others in your life saying, "You could have a boyfriend right now if you wanted one." For whatever reason, you're not feeling it. You hurt that person with your lack of interest just as much as others have hurt you. It's a bad cycle.

There are some who enjoy the interests of many people, even if they're not interested in any of them. I am not that person. I don't enjoy it when people are interested in me who I know are not right for me. I've had a few guys tell me they can't be friends with me anymore because of it. I understand that feeling. As much as it's happened to me, I hate doing it to other people. Sometimes, I don't understand why it's so hard to find two compatible people who are right for each other and feel the same way.

#8 Hazard of Singlehood: The Endless, Unanswered Question

I don't know about you, but one thing that drives me crazy about being single is the unknown. Who am I going to marry? Is it this guy? Is it that guy? If I date this person here and he's the wrong one, am I delaying my pairing with the right guy? What if the right guy is in my life and because of my impatience that our relationship hasn't begun, I'm diving into something different? Will he get discouraged and give up? There are two questions God has refused to answer with certainty for me: who and when. In the chapter on foreshadowing, we'll talk about why it's probably best He doesn't answer those.

#9 Hazard of Singlehood: Facing Love Interests Who Are Now With Others

Once you're married, this problem hopefully lessens or goes away. One area I struggle with is seeing people I've liked with girls they're clearly interested in, or other girlfriends, dates, or wives. I have a hard time with what Satan loves to throw in my face: "You are never the choice. Guys will always choose someone else." Running into those who've moved on while you are still alone can hurt.

#10 Hazard of Singlehood: Vulnerability

I had a dream one night of a man breaking into my house to attack me. Right before I woke up, I shouted Jesus' name. I woke up in a panic and couldn't go back to sleep for the rest of the night. Naturally, those are disconcerting nights to wake up in bed alone, especially when you live by yourself.

When my father was sick and I feared losing him, I thought

heavily about how the loss of him would be different for my sister than for me. She was married and having children. She wouldn't feel as alone. Our parents are the main family I have. Vulnerability gets to me sometimes.

One night, when I was sick, a guy called and said he was going to the drugstore to get me some meds so I could sleep. As soon as we hung up, I cried. The gesture meant the world to me; it was so foreign. I was so used to taking care of myself that such a kind gesture tore into my heart. I thought back to a night when I was sick a year earlier. I couldn't stop coughing for hours. I had to leave my apartment about one thirty in the morning to find an all-night drugstore to get cough syrup. I cried so much that night, feeling so alone.

Have you had nights like this? The same thing happens when our cars break down or we can't figure out how to open jars by ourselves. We don't have that partner there to help. Just know that you are not alone in having those moments of vulnerability.

Well, those are some of the hazards of singlehood. I am just trying to be honest about it. Does knowing you are not alone in how you feel bring comfort? My hope for those who read this is to remember to be sensitive to your other single friends, too. If there's an area of sensitivity here that isn't necessarily a bother to you, remember it may be a source of pain for other single friends. Do your best to reach out to them and not make life more "hazardous" than it already feels sometimes. Remember, in a later chapter, we will look at all the benefits we have as single people as well!

CHAPTER EIGHT
God, This is Taking Forever! Did You Fall Asleep On the Job?

WANTED:
A strong lawyer willing to take on a formidable, unbending,
always-right defendant:

<u>Claimant</u>: *Cheryl McKay*
<u>The Accused</u>: *God*
<u>Grounds</u>: *Breach of contract, misrepresentation, and falsification of promises.*
<u>Evidence</u>: *Jesus said, "Ask, and it shall be given you." I asketh for a husband; I receiveth him not. Jesus also said I could say to a mountain "move" and it would fall into the sea. I've commanded whatever this mountain is that stands tall between my husband and me to get lost. Vamoose. Disappear. Apparently, it did not take a hike into the Pacific, the Atlantic, especially not the Arctic Ocean. I still don't see him in front of me. I see nothing but an insurmountable mountain. Kilimanjaro-like. Jesus also declared that if two of us agree on earth in prayer, it shall be done. Well, I can introduce attendee lists into evidence of the bazillion groups of two or more who've prayed for me to have a husband. Despite all of us being in agreement, it has not come to pass. Don't even get me started on the evidence I can drum up about having faith the size of a mustard seed. Seriously, two millimeters in diameter. Even at my lowest, most faithless moments, I at least have that.*

GOD'S REBUTTAL:
The God Who Needs No Lawyer
(Please note the following are purely for comic relief:)

- *You twist my Scripture.*
- *You make fun of My precious verse about allowing patience to have her perfect work. Look it up. It's James 1:4 (in case you forgot).*
- *You don't see "The Big Picture."*
- *You don't understand how I define "My best."*
- *You jump to conclusions when you hear the word "soon."*
- *You forget that just because a promise remains unfulfilled doesn't mean I've breached that promise. It means it's not time.*
- *Every time I discuss this promise with you, you assume I'm bringing it up because the time has changed to "now."*
- *Stop eating so much chocolate just because you're lonely. It's not good for the "temple" I gave you.*
- *You can't find Me in contempt.*
- *I don't need to show up in court because I don't need to defend Myself.*

Wait.

That's got to be my least favorite word God uses, and yet, He uses it a lot. It characterizes almost my entire life. Its meaning monopolizes many of my prayers to God. It's the most common answer He gives to many prayers. No amount of pleading makes Him change the season.

The page. The chapter.

Even though I don't think we need to arrive at some place of perfection before God can deliver a husband, our waiting might be because of us. Sometimes, there are ways in which God needs to work in us before we'll be ready for marriage. Some causes of delay were discussed in earlier chapters. This chapter will discuss delays we may be responsible for. For example, delays can be caused by impatience, racing ahead of God and into counterfeit love stories, jealousy, having false expectations, anger against God or mistrust, or stealing the pen back from God (a.k.a. taking back control) when we think He's doing nothing.

TOP REASONS CHERYL SHOULDN'T HAVE TO WAIT ANY LONGER:

1. *She doesn't want to.*
2. *She's already clocked thirty-something years of waiting. Been there, done that.*
3. *Jesus might come back soon, and she doesn't want to die a virgin.*
4. *She's believed steadily in this promise for many years.*
5. *She believes she's ready.*

Patience, My Dear

As mentioned, I sometimes dislike one of the verses God loves to remind me of: "But let patience have her perfect work, that ye may be perfect and entire, wanting nothing" (James 1:4, kjv).

In Summer 2004, I was on my way to visit my sister. She was pregnant with her first child. At the airport, my Bible class reading included James 1:4. This was the beginning of me getting sick of that verse. When I got to my sister's, my mother and I were fixing up the nursery for my soon-to-be nephew, Jake. I was excited for my sister, but sad for me taking yet another family trip alone, still not having my own family. Silently, while peeling wallpaper, I cried out to God in my spirit: *Lord, when will it be my turn? When will I get to come on these family trips and finally have my teammate?*

My mother responded to my *silent* thought: "Let patience have her perfect work." I rolled my eyes at the wall in response, so she didn't see me. Yes, I can be a pain. Then I said, "Mom, what made you say that?" She replied, "I don't know. I just heard it." Yes, you just heard it because God whispered it to you to respond to me and my impatient, private moaning! Well, I'm sorry, but I'm not patient and I don't want for nothing!

A few days later, God sent me a dream. I called it "When Passions Met Patience." I title my dreams like movie titles because I feel like some dreams are mini-movies written by God with specific messages for us. The dream involved me racing through the set of the soap opera *Passions* looking for a script supervisor named Patience. Doesn't take a genius to figure out the message God sent.

There were lots symbols within the dream about racing ahead into the wrong things in the wrong order. If you remember from the first dream I shared in this book, script supervisors only track scripts. They do not write them. God wanted to move me from passions to patience and did not want me to write my own story. Yes, God does have a sense of humor sometimes when He lovingly corrects me.

To say "waiting is hard" is the understatement of the century. If you're reading this book, you're likely getting just as impatient as I am for God to write this love story. While waiting is hard, again, I'd take waiting alone over being with the wrong person in the interim any day. Wouldn't you rather wait for God's best than end up with a bunch of counterfeits along the way?

Cheryl's Journal (Summer 2004)

Cheryl's prayer: It says in Psalm 33:4 that God's Word is right and true, that He is faithful in all that He does. I need to believe God and trust He has my best interests at heart, no matter what He allows to happen in my life. God, I already know rushing ahead of You spells disaster. I want the relationship You've promised. I don't even begin to understand what is taking so long and why You can't get him — whoever he is — to cooperate with You. The story You're writing is the ultimate exercise in surrender for me. I'm helpless. I'm a viewer. Is there any adjustment I need? Anything I'm doing wrong, Lord?

God's reply: I don't want you to fill in blanks or make assumptions. I want you to take My promises and believe them regardless of how circumstances look or feel to you at the time. I want you to believe in Me, no matter how long I take to fulfill a word for you. Trust that I have your best interests at heart. I know your heart and know your reactions and feelings. I know your future and what's to come. If only you could see this how I see it. Trust Me. That's all you have to do. Don't worry about timing and who and where and how. Rest in Me and let Me allow things to unfold when I deem ready. It's hard to believe a promise in the midst of pain, but that's what I ask you to do anyway. To believe despite what circumstances may tell you. That is true faith.

No Counterfeits, Please

What if God intends to bring the right person, but just before this happens, you are distracted by a man on whom you know God has not placed His stamp of approval? You decide you're tired of waiting. You don't realize God is about to make the right introduction. You dive into this relationship because you're lonely. The likely outcome is that you'll enjoy the attention and forget about God's story for a while. You may even find ways to justify this as God's story. However, eventually it starts to fall apart because it wasn't built by God.

Five months down the road, you realize you wasted all this time with the wrong person and you have to extract yourself—or the guy dumps you. It hurts. The guy may have made you feel better temporarily, but now you're paying the price. It's been a five-month delay so far. Tack onto that the time you need to heal and be restored by God from this counterfeit.

Meanwhile, God has to put the right guy on hold because of your behavior. Who knows what mistakes he might make in his own impatience, waiting on God to bring him his wife? I believe this is where our freewill can get in the way. The hope is those right matches will be made, but the freewill of two people and their cooperation with God's plan plays a role in how long we wait. While people like to believe God is ultimately in control, we can mess things up along the way to His best.

The Green-Eyed Monster

Let's look at a big issue for many of us: jealousy.

In 2006, I decided to find a new place of ministry, especially after I'd experienced a disappointment with a guy I liked. A friend of mine invited me to a Bible study she said was great except she was one of the only single girls there. Most others were married or engaged.

Did I mention all these couples were in their early twenties? I was already in my thirties. I was the oldest one there. Upon my arrival, I wanted nothing more than to leave and yet, God caught my attention with this Bible study. It was meaty, not for the faint-of-heart Christian and not for one who wasn't interested in growing in the Lord. Something drew me to stay, despite the demographics. There's nothing more frustrating than being in pain over the loss of a candidate and finding yourself surrounded by people ten years younger who are already married.

I found myself asking God, "What are they doing that I'm not doing? Why do they get to have this? Were they more prepared than I am? Is that why you blessed them with marriage and not me?" It didn't make sense at all. The study was so awesome, and I was growing every week in the Lord. So I made myself stay, despite my discomfort. It was an important part of my life and my growth with God for a long season of time. I'm thankful God helped me look past my issues and allowed me to grow there, and then share what I've learned with other people. God wanted me in a Bible study because of God Himself, not because I was hoping to meet a guy there.

Do you ever begrudge the blessings God brings into someone else's life? This is something God tested me in, through this group. I had to learn to be there and not resent younger couples. If you struggle with jealousy (a.k.a. coveting), this may be something God would like to clean up before this blessing can come to you. Take an honest look at yourself. Test your reactions when you meet other couples. This was a weakness I had to overcome. It's also not something you deal with and get over. It seems like it can come up, again and again, as friends get engaged or married.

One time, I counseled a girl who believed a particular guy would be her husband. It didn't seem like she was right about this, and I encouraged her to let this go. I spent time praying for her tender heart over this issue. When I heard this man got engaged to someone else, I checked in to see how she was doing. Her response surprised me. She was fine because God had sent her a new boyfriend. My internal jaw dropped. I can unequivocally tell you God has never done that for me. Never! I've had to watch more than one love interest, more than one boyfriend move on without a single thought of me while I go five plus years between dates. Knowing how delicate she was, I was thankful God gave her this grace. I'll admit it ticked me off that it's not a grace He's ever extended to me.

The same thing happened during my year of depression after a big break up. I couldn't figure out how to get myself out of the deep hole I felt stuck in. I went to a friend who I knew battled depression in the past. I asked her, "How did God help you out of that pit?" Her answer was, "God sent me my husband." During her depression, the man she ended up marrying saw her emotional state, took her on as a case for prayer, showed up as often as she needed support, and eventually won her heart. She believed God's grace brought this man into her life at the right time. In essence, she feels her husband—as God's blessing—rescued her. But again, there I was with open, festering wounds. As month after month went by, they weren't getting better. God was in no way sending me my husband to help me climb out of it.

It's so difficult to watch God give certain blessings to some people and not others. I can say I know I am a stronger person now. God didn't give me that person during my pain—God alone walked me through it.

In *Never the Bride*, I tackled this issue through an assignment God gives to my lead character Jessie. She's been writing her love story fantasies in her journals her whole life with her purple pen, including all the creative ways a guy could propose to her. God asks her to give away these ideas to other people. Yes, God wants her to spend her days watching other women get what she wants most. She opens a business, staging proposals for guys who want to pop the question to their women. Jessie didn't want to be the person who hurt while watching other people get what she wants, but through her business, she faces this in herself.

I have the feeling that once God lets me know what story He's writing, I will be able to see where His hand was at work during those dark times. I'm sure He was at work when I thought He was doing nothing. As God once told me, "This is not a script you can write nor cast." So far, God has kept the cast list confidential—a cast of one name. Much of God's work happens behind the scenes. You know how on movie DVDs, you can watch behind-the-scenes footage? God doesn't release that footage until after the story is told, when His movie is finished and screened.

Expect the Expected

Let's talk about expectations. If God hasn't revealed something specific to you, you shouldn't be standing on the belief it will definitely happen. If God has revealed a specific promise but not the "when," don't stand on your own timeline. Expectations set us up for disappointment. I can't tell you how many times I started a new year in January, declaring: *This is it! This is the year!* Every year ended the same: no husband. Had God told me that would be the year? No. If I thought He did, I was usually wrong or had added my words to what God said.

I was told in 2007, by one with a supposed prophetic gift, that my relationship would start by the end of the year. When that year came and went with no budding romance, I realized my definition of "start" might vastly differ from God's. For all I know, I may have started an important friendship that year that will turn into something more in the future. Until I know God's answer to the "who," I can't tell you whether that prophetic word was correct. I don't fault prophetic people for mistakes. They're human; they are not always going to be right. Sometimes, people may be expressing their hopes for you, not realizing it. So, I try not to place too much stock in a particular word, especially not when it includes a time frame and is unconfirmed in other ways.

If you stand on a false expectation and it doesn't come to pass, you can find yourself angry with God because of it. This is a recipe for delay.

HEADLINE:

The Patience-Deficient Screenwriter Cheryl McKay Campaigns to Have the Following Words and Phrases Taken Out of God's Dictionary When it Comes to Her Love Life:

Wait, Don't Walk, Stop, Door Closed, Door Slammed, Turn Around, Not Now, No, Tarry, Pause, Dilly Dally, Linger, Procrastinate, Postpone.

When God Seems to be Snoring

My biggest crisis of faith moment came when I had to do my first interview for *Never the Bride,* the novel version. A columnist asked me where I got the idea for the story and from where my lead character came. For the first time, I found myself publicly answering questions with words like, "My lead character, Jessie, is based on me. The story is inspired by my friendship with God and my belief that God cares enough about our love lives to write our love stories."

Ah! I freaked.

In my personal life, God hasn't done this yet and here I am, putting out both a screenplay and a novel with a story claiming He does. Yet, I have no proof God does this! Yeah, maybe I have other people's stories collected that I believe are about God's divine love matches, but what proof do I have in my own life? I'm vowing to the world that God does something He hasn't bothered to do for me! (Yet. Yet. Yet.) I had a meltdown over that. I thought: *This is just the beginning of these kinds of questions. Can I tell people this character is based on me when my character has her happy ending and I don't?*

Yes, that's exactly what God wants me to do. After I calmed down and took some time to pray, I felt like God said, "Yes, you can. That's the point. That's faith! People will relate to you a lot more if in the beginning of sharing this story you don't have what you want and yet you believe Me anyway." Ugh! Seriously? I asked, "God, are you hanging me out on a limb?"

I'll admit it; this is scary. I wrote the script based on God's prompting to do so. I knew He called me to share the story. Then He prompted me to sell the story idea as a novel and team up with my wonderful friend, Rene Gutteridge, who's brilliant at penning novelized versions of screenplays. Then He led me to write this book in faith—while still alone—sharing He will do this if we trust Him!

When I sit in a place of disbelief or mistrust in God, I can cause my own delays. It says in Psalms 84:11b (kjv), "…no good thing will He withhold from them that walk uprightly." If God is withholding what we desire, it's because, for now, it is not a good thing for us. So, is God asleep on the job of setting up my love story? Quite the opposite. He is at work: it just happens to be behind the scenes.

Cheryl's Journal (2004)
> *God: Believe Me, believe Me despite circumstances. Believe Me in the face of all My enemy will try to say and whisper. I reward belief. You've had to believe for a long time for your precious promises. A long time by your definition of time. In My realm, you've been waiting for the right amount of time. That will continue until that perfect moment. That moment in time I deem as right and pure and lovely and good enough for My daughter. You will not regret this time you've waited. You will see and understand My purpose. Believe! Continue to believe.*

Sick Heart Over Here, Lord

Sometimes our mistrust can cause us to lose hope; we despair over our circumstances. Do you ever use Bible verses to tell God how He should behave? I've often tried to talk to God about Proverbs 13:12, about hope deferred, like in the following entry:

Cheryl's Journal (2006)
> *Lord, you recognize that a hope deferred makes the heart sick. So why do You still have me wait? Why do You let me hope? Can't You do something to fix this or progress this? My heart aches with loneliness, disappointment, and a hope that keeps getting brutally shattered. I feel like a fool at times, the way I cling to hope. I am always hoping. I don't know how my hope stays so alive when such a small fraction of what I hope for happens. I'm grieved over how often this happens to me. Am I just refusing to get the point? Have You sent a different message and I'm just not getting it? At the same time, I don't think You've ever had a different message about this situation. The only part that doesn't line up is reality.*

I wondered for so long why God recognizes that deferred hopes make the heart sick, and yet, He still tarries. Then I felt like He offered me wisdom about this. A hope is not deferred until you've given up on it. That's what makes the heart sick. If you trust and believe in what God told you, no matter how long you have to wait for Him to give it to you, then your hopes won't derail you emotionally.

Remember: God understands the pain of waiting.

Persnickety Persistence

In Luke 18, Jesus tells the parable of the persistent widow. The purpose of this parable was for Jesus to tell His disciples why they should not give up on praying. There's an interesting, seeming contradiction in verse 7–8a, kjv: "And shall not God avenge His own elect, which cry day and night unto Him, though He bear long with them? I tell you that He will avenge them speedily." It says God bears long with His people but avenges speedily. How can that be true? It's not a contradiction. It's referring to how God can make us wait a long time, but when He shows up with an answer, He shows up mightily and swiftly.

It reminds me of my years of praying for God to take care of my professional life. The day God showed up with *The Ultimate Gift* was a day all those prayers were answered. My dream had arrived after one follow-up meeting. I know and trust that God can do the same with our love lives.

Our wait may have nothing to do with us. As stated already, it may simply mean it's not the right time. Habakkuk reminds us to wait on God: "For the vision is yet for an appointed time, but at the end it shall speak, and not lie: though it tarry, wait for it; because it will surely come, it will not tarry." (Habakkuk 2:3, kjv). This is another verse that seems contradictory. It lingers and yet the answer comes without delay. God is this enigma sometimes, isn't He?

You don't have to make Jesus your boyfriend before you can have a husband, but you do need to wait on God for His perfect timing. Only He knows why you're still waiting. Don't be afraid to ask if there is anything you're doing wrong that's causing your delay. As I've mentioned, before 2004, I wouldn't have been ready. God knew what He was doing when He thwarted my attempts to move that side of my life forward. I had lots of emotional issues that needed God's healing touch. Ever since He finished performing that heart surgery, my job has been to wait on Him. (And wait. And wait.)

> *Cheryl's Journal (06/06/04)*
>
> *God: You are not moving backwards. Didn't I tell you I'm moving you forward swiftly? I know you question My timing and what "soon" really means. Daughter, you are not alone in that. It's one of the most common questions I field. I have many impatient children. I understand the ache in your soul more than you can comprehend — the desire to be loved fully. The ache you feel for one is the ache I feel over billions from every generation. No human is capable of loving Me freely and fully in the way I yearn to be loved. It just can't be until My fallen world is straightened. That day will come. I long for that day more than any, yet I, too, have to wait a little longer to give as many a chance to choose Me as possible.*

CHAPTER NINE

God, Have You Ever Heard of Foreshadowing? (Just Give Me a Little Hint!)

FACEBOOK STATUS:
God tells me things on a need-to-know basis.
Apparently, He doesn't think I need to know anything.
God has my pen. I've seen no real hints lately.

In storytelling, there's a concept called *foreshadowing*. It's a device that writers use to plant seeds about things to come. You watch a scene at the beginning of a movie that you don't fully understand until you get to its end. Then, you wonder how on earth you missed what was coming. That piece of foreshadowing hinted what's to come, but you couldn't see the big picture.

I can't even begin to count how many times I've asked God to give me some hint — or movie preview — of what He's up to. *Come on, Lord. How about one hint? Seriously. You can trust me with the information.* Hmm. Can He really?

God is the Master Storyteller. It's likely — with your love story —

He's laced clues and hints along the way that you can't recognize yet. It's one of those things that may just pay off after the fact. That's because God doesn't want you to know your whole future in advance. He may give you pieces to hold on to, perhaps, if you are short on hope. He isn't likely to tell you everything up front. We may think knowing more is what we want, but is it in our best interests?

There are many times I wanted God to talk to me about where we were in the story. *Lord, are we still stuck in Act One? Have we moved on to Act Two? Are we about to hit that crisis moment before the story turns from Act Two to Act Three? You know, the same Act Three where the two lovers finally get together? Because I feel like I'm having a crisis over here!*

We Prophesy in Part

I've mentioned that God was clear with me: He supplied the prophetic promise that, one day, I would get married. It came when I needed that promise to hold on to. As mentioned, God didn't tell me who or when. There were many times I wanted those two pieces of information. I've had arguments (usually one-sided) with God about this. *"Lord, if You tell me who, I won't date the wrong people. If You tell me when, I won't sit here wanting something long before You have it ready for me."* Apparently, God doesn't buy that argument. I don't know why; it seems sound to me. God knows better than to share those details with me — at least not to share it in a way that I understand what He means just yet.

> *Cheryl's Journal (06/12/07)*
> *The parable about the seeds in Mark 4 reminds me of prophetic words. We can hear prophetic words, but Satan can try to steal them before they have a chance to grow into fruition. We sometimes believe for these words, for a time or we receive with a joy that wears off quickly. Boy, do I know how that feels! God doesn't want me to lose faith even though He supplied those words to me a long time ago. He wants me to believe even in the face of no evidence that He's at work.*

Do you think that if you decide to trust God with the pen and let Him write your story that He is somehow obligated to give you a sense of what He's up to? Do you petition God to tell you the who, what, where, when, why, and how? I believe God will supply slices of this information. I think it can be harmful for us to know too much too soon. Here's why:

It was a good thing God told me one day I'd get married. However, let me share a problem with you about this. Let's say a year goes by. Nothing has changed in my personal life. I go to a prayer meeting and another person prophesizes, "Cheryl, one day you're going to get married and have a family." Confirmation is good. It's always nice to have more than one source for the same information.

Then another year goes by. I end up at a different prayer meeting. A woman there gives me the verse Psalm 68:6, where it talks about God putting lonely people in families. Considering I already have my parents and my sister's family in my life, and I'm still lonely, obviously this is referring to the family I don't have yet. However, hearing this gets my excitement up. In fact, every prophetic reminder from God kicks up hope.

This is not hypothetical; this is what happened to me. Do you see where this can become problematic? On one hand, it's encouraging to hear God hasn't forgotten me or His promise, but the continuing reminders also became a source of pain.

Let's say I am in a season of time where the absence of a husband isn't on my mind that much. Then, I receive a reminder or confirmation of this promise to come. My dormant desire kicks up like wildfire and, suddenly, I can't stand the wait. Each time God brought it up, I felt like that meant the time was imminent. But "now" still hasn't come. I call this the "Disney World Effect."

After years of this going on, I hit a point where I just didn't want to hear about it anymore. It reminded me of how Abraham went through this. God would give him a promise, not deliver it yet, and come back with the same promise using a different illustration—like the number of grains of sand or number of stars. I wondered why Abraham didn't just say, "Enough already! Either deliver the promise or stop reminding me because it's too painful." That's how I felt. So, I asked God to stop talking about it:

Cheryl's Journal (2007)
> *Lord, it's fine if You don't want to deliver this promise to me now. I get it. It's not the right time. Your constant reminders of the promise are hurting me more than they help. It kicks up my desire for the promise and when it doesn't happen, it just hurts me more. It reminds me of what it would be like for a father to promise to take his child to Disney World. The kid is bound to get excited, his eyes wide with anticipation. That child wants to go now, as soon as the promise is made. Every day he's made to wait feels like a year. After a while, the child's excitement may die down. That is, until the father brings it up again, promising to take him. But if the father promises and continues to not deliver, the child will grow disillusioned. That's how I feel. I know You're faithful. I know You mean it when You make a promise. I feel like the kid You keep promising to take to Disney World, but You don't. Not so far. Would You tell a kid for five years about this trip if You intended to make the child wait that long?*

I poured out my heart to the God I know can take my honesty. It didn't mean He stopped reminding me about the promise or speaking to me through dreams about my future marriage.

In early 2008, a woman who just met me prayed with me. As she started to pray for those hurts in my heart about not being married, she said, "God is not the Father who promises to take his kid to Disney World and doesn't do it."

Whoa!

I knew God was speaking. He heard what I said when I poured

out my honesty to Him. Here He was, bringing it up with someone who didn't know me or understand how much pain existed over not having the promised blessings.

> Cheryl's Journal (06/18/05)
>
> If I get a dream, it makes the desire for the promise too strong. If I don't get dreams, my desire to hear more through dreams is too strong. Nothing about this works; nothing about this doesn't hurt me. What is the answer here? What will make this painful situation more livable for me?

Do Not Awaken Love Before the Right Time

There's another detriment to knowing too much too soon. Consider this verse: "Daughters of Jerusalem, I charge you by the gazelles and by the does of the field: Do not arouse or awaken love until it so desires." (Song of Solomon 2:7.)

Let's say back in 2003, God told me the identity of the person I was going to marry. Can you imagine what it would be like now, years later, if I'd known all this time and the guy still didn't? That would have been ridiculously hard—to watch that person not cooperate with God or date other people, while I waited faithfully for him. Also, I'd be developing feelings for a person who has no reason to love me yet, if the time wasn't right. I'd be waking up love too early. How hard would it be to behave normally around that man? How could I not come across as hurt every time he "cheated" on me or did something to walk further away from God's plan for us? Think of the control it would take to not slap the guy over the head for taking so long to play his divine role in God's script!

There are many times I've asked God to tell me when. I'd reason, "Lord, even if it's not for a long time, at least I could temper my hopes if You don't intend to give this to me anytime soon." But I'll admit I'm glad, when God reminded me in 2003 I'd get married one day, that I had no idea God's promise involved many more years of waiting. I may not have been encouraged enough by that promise to deal with the pain I faced in that break up.

My main point here is that God, in His wisdom, knows how much clarity or foreshadowing we need. We need to trust Him to give us just the right amount. If we focus on trying to figure out every single clue God gives us, our eyes are on the "prize" and not on Jesus. If anything, that makes our vision fuzzy. One time, God said to me, "When you try to figure out how all the pieces I've given fit together, what does that feel like to you? How has it been working out so far?" Ouch! He was right. He just wants us to remain in a place of thankfulness for what we have and what's ahead, even if we can't see it with our natural eyes.

You'll Find the God Tracks

I do believe that once you find out what God is writing for the romantic-comedy script of your life, you will be able to look back and trace clues, winks, nods, and hints. I know that each path God weaves is intricate. You will have a story to tell. You may not realize what part you're playing *as* you're playing it. God may shield your eyes from seeing everything clearly until the right time. Trust that He is at work, even when His foreshadowing fingers are not making themselves known. You want to be on the same page as the one God is writing, not twenty script pages ahead or behind.

Remember! God is not above making a promise—showing you what's to come—then making you wait a long time for it. Just ask Sarah. Joseph. Daniel. We're in good company. Sometimes, when we hear a promise from God, we assume the promise fulfillment is next. Often, God gives us that word so we won't get too discouraged when what happens next is the opposite, like a breakup.

At a prayer meeting, a woman saw a picture (or vision) of me with an engagement ring. She didn't see the guy in this picture, just the ring and my hand. I wrongly assumed, since God gave her this picture while I was in the midst of a relationship, that God was revealing I would end up marrying this particular guy. It was the moment I gave myself permission to fall in love with him because it felt safe. The man wasn't in the vision. I filled in the wrong blanks. I paid a painful price for it! God gave that picture to encourage me about the future, not because it had anything to do with that guy. God knew that guy was about to break my heart just a few months later.

One day at a church, a pastor gave a wonderful illustration of this. He talked about how, when God supplies a promise, it may feel like the promise is right in front of you. Sometimes, God puts you in a slingshot and pulls back on the band. You suddenly feel like you're moving away from the promise, not closer. You calculate it: "I was so close and now it looks like I'm months away from the promise." Then God pulls the band back more. In your eyes, it seems like you're even further away and you cry out, "God, now I'm two years away from this!" So you doubt God. Some people, during this time, crawl out of the slingshot because they lose their faith. God uses this method so, when the right time comes and He lets go of the rubber band, it immediately thrusts you forward rapidly into what He has for you. That's how Joseph, in a flash, went from prison to helping run a country.

Cheryl's Journal (09/09/05)

Are God's promises ever conditional? Do my reactions and my obedience to His promises matter? Are there precedents in God's Word for someone losing a promise because of his or her choices? How about because of someone else's disobedience and freewill? In Moses' time, their promises took so long to happen because of their grumbling and complaining and wandering in the desert. It didn't have to be that way. Their travels could have taken less than two weeks. Instead, it took forty years to arrive at the Promised Land. That's not because God was unfaithful to His promise. It's because of the people's unbelief, grumbling, and complaining. So many of those who were promised the land died before they made it there, and the promise went to the next generation. They constantly questioned God's love and heart toward them. They didn't believe He had their best interests at heart. This grieved God. That didn't stop Him from doing as promised. Moses didn't get to enter the Promised Land because of his defiance striking a rock. This does tell me that my behavior matters. Some promises can be set aside. In Numbers 20:12, God reprimanded Moses for not trusting Him.

Don't Let a Promise Become an Idol

Another warning about "foreshadowing" is this: don't let God's promises become too important to you. If we place too much importance on something God reveals and we care more about the promise than God, He may not be able to trust us with that blessing. He may withhold until it's no longer an idol. Remember in Genesis where God tested Abraham? After twenty-five years worth of promises about Isaac, God asked Abraham to give Isaac up and sacrifice him. Seems crazy, doesn't it? It was a test Abraham passed. He would withhold nothing from God. God rewarded his faithfulness. He also made the promise sound conditional to Abraham's obedience. Genesis 22:16b–17a, reads, "because you have done this and have not withheld your son, your only son, I will surely bless you and make your descendants as numerous as the stars in the sky and as the sand on the seashore." Remember both of those illustrations were used during the twenty-five years when Abraham waited for God to fulfill that promise. Here, God speaks after the promise was fulfilled and Isaac was already born! God made it clear that the promise of many descendents could happen, now that Abraham didn't hold back Isaac for himself. Abraham showed God that God came first.

God's Protection

Sometimes, God flashes a glaring red light. God might speak up about your future mate to protect you if you're about to walk into the wrong love story, one He isn't writing for you. God might supply direction because He knows you're about to be tempted by the wrong person in your vulnerable state of loneliness. For example, God may supply a dream that tells you something specific about the person you should be on the lookout for, just before the wrong guy is about to walk into your life—one who doesn't have that quality. When God does reveal details to you, don't fall into the temptation to try to fit someone into what God says. When we're lonely and impatient, we can fall into the trap of trying to get anyone to be the payoff to this love story God's writing. I've been in danger of that many times myself. I trust that when it's God, we'll know it. We won't have to question or reason away certain details because they don't match what God has revealed.

When I ask people why they think I'm still waiting for love, I almost always get the same answer: "God is protecting you. God has a protective fence around your heart. God has blinded the wrong men to you." If I step out from behind that fence on my own too soon, it's the equivalent of stepping into oncoming traffic. (Ever played Frogger? Splat!)

We should welcome and ask for this protection. There are many godly women in bad marriages, going through trials no woman should have to face—including facing Christian husbands cheating on them. Some of my friends who had, or currently are in, bad marriages will readily admit they did not wait for God's approval before they walked down the aisle. They would never declare they are in (or getting out of) "God-written love stories." They often admit they raced into marriage because of sex, convenience, and various reasons without asking God how He felt. Or they admit they may have said God told them it was right at the time, when He never did, and they were just hearing what they wanted to hear. They give me a wake up call. Not waiting on God's best can have dire and lasting consequences. They remind me to be thankful that I am alone, not facing what these women face.

I am not saying every difficult marriage is the result of stepping out of God's will or not waiting on God's love story. Even in the best, God-written love stories, there can be difficult seasons.

God loves us dearly. We are His treasured daughters. He only wants the best men for His daughters. We need to love God first, not His words and promises, and not the love story He is weaving on our behalf.

Just wait to see what words He will write on that page.

A Foreshadowing Dream (07/12/06)

There's a pool party in my honor at an indoor, in-ground pool. It also has wave-like activity at the edges you'd see at a beach. I did not plan this party. Someone else did. It was set up as a surprise for me. There are people from work and my Bible study group here. This party has been thrown as a fund-raiser, gift-giving party for me because of losses I've suffered. It's as though someone shared a list of what I lost because of toxic mold. People are coming to celebrate me, bringing gifts. I see a check on a table. The check memo line says "For Christmas and photo losses." I watch friends playing in the pool. Everyone is having fun. I see a guy who's a friend of mine, and watch him play around. I'm surprised this many people showed up for my party. At first, I feel like someone's going to throw me in the water — given that I am the guest of honor and I'm in a bathing suit. I hover at the wall a bit, laughing at everyone. I wonder if the water is cold, but then I realize the water is warm and get in on my own. I swim near the guy and we start playing around, having fun and flirting. We put our arms around each other's necks, looking at each other closely. I'm surprised by my new interest in him.

Cheryl's Prayer about the Dream: Lord, I feel like this dream is to encourage me that love is coming. I seriously doubt my husband is the same person in this dream. I imagine he's being used as a symbol as the type of guy who was willing to answer Your call and help me during my losses. He was the payoff to one of the most dynamic prophetic dreams You ever gave me, helping me when I needed it. So, I'm sure that's why You cast him in that role in this dream. Because You cast this man, I can only assume the man You have for me will be one who hears Your voice and listens to Your call. That's encouraging. Since my interest in this man takes me by surprise as someone I already knew but wasn't originally interested in, maybe I know the guy and just don't realize who he is yet.

I feel like You've used the symbolism of my losses to speak to me about how You know I feel I've lost lots of time. Because of my history, there's been heartache in this area of life. This includes my continuing sadness about spending every Christmas without this man, and every birthday, which happens to be so close to Christmas. I'm sure that's why Christmas was written on the restoration check. I believe You're telling me You are taking care of this and You will restore this part of my life. You often remind me You have only "good gifts" for Your daughter. This dream reminds me of the same. Thank You, Father.

CHAPTER TEN

God, Would You Go Wake Up My Husband
and Tell Him to Come Find Me?

Cheryl's Journal (09/05/04)
God, would You please go chase after that
husband of mine and stand at the foot of his bed,
and yell at him? Tell him he has a wife who's in
pain because he hasn't come to find her yet. Tell
him to rescue me.

I kept and dated that prayer, wondering if one day when I compare notes with my husband – if he happens to also keep journals – he might have recorded a bizarre experience that night. A frightening, angelic visit. A strange dream. A haunting voice from the galaxy telling him to get with God's program.

Do you spend time praying for your future husband? Are your prayers just angry prayers because of what's missing in your life based on your needs? Have you consciously tried to pray for his well-being, future, and preparation for being your husband?

I hear that once we are married, it's going to be about loving and serving that other person. Maybe we should start getting used to this now by praying selfless prayers for our future mates, even if we don't know who we're praying for. We will need to employ the same practice once married. Instead of just being frustrated with them for not showing up yet, we can love them by using our energy toward prayers that accomplish much in the Spirit realm.

Remember when I discussed the insights God gave me about why He won't dull my desire for a husband? There was another reason: He knew my pain charged my prayers for my missing husband. If I didn't desire his arrival, then I wouldn't have a reason to pray for his life, his walk with God, and his journey toward me. That's why I've devoted a chapter in this book to praying power prayers for the future mate that hasn't show up yet.

Prayer Points for Our Future Husbands

Here are some potential topics you can cover in your prayers for your husband. Obviously you don't need to do them all in one prayer session. You can focus on whichever ones you feel led to pray at the time:

1. Pray for his walk with God, that he continues to grow spiritually and is prepped to be the spiritual head of a household, and that he makes God the top priority in his life.

2. Pray for his ability to hear God's voice, for his ear to be in tune to hear all of God's instructions.

3. Pray for his will to be bendable toward whatever God wants for his life.

4. Pray for his emotional health—that any past wounds be dealt with and healed. Pray for restoration in all areas.

5. Pray for his physical health.

6. Pray that he break free of any unhealthy addictions, if needed.

7. Pray for his career, his life's work, that he be established in the field where God wants to use him and that he be wise with his resources.

8. Pray for his ministry—that he be sensitive to God's call on his life when it comes to ministering to and serving others. Also, pray for God to prepare both of you for the ways you will minister together.

9. Pray for his preparation—that he yields to all that God's potter's hands would like to accomplish in him.

10. Pray for God to send any trials necessary into his life that will allow the preparation process to be complete. I realize that may be a bit controversial. Knowing how much God has accomplished in my life through trials, I would expect nothing less of my husband's journey toward me.

11. Pray for God to prepare him to be a father, if the two of you will ultimately raise a family together.

12. Pray for God to help him be responsible with his finances and prepare him to be a significant contributor and provider to the household.

13. Pray for his identity as a man, his masculinity and self-esteem, that he grows into the man God wants him to be.

14. Pray for him to not be distracted by any counterfeits—especially other women that God doesn't intend to use for his growth.

15. Pray for God to allow this man to see you the way God wants you to be seen, with God's heart toward you.

16. Pray for God to show you how to pray for your husband. Be open to whatever His Spirit may whisper to you, to cover your husband's needs. If you feel God gives you something specific, write it down and date it. Save it for later.

Pray in the Spirit

This isn't the book to teach about praying in the Spirit (also known as praying in tongues). If this is something you are interested in, I encourage you to read my friend Susan Rohrer's book, THE HOLY SPIRIT: *Amazing Power for Everyday People.*

For those who do pray in the Spirit, one prayer I love to pray is, "Lord, I'd like to intercede for my future husband right now. Only you know his deepest needs. Spirit, please make intercession on his behalf through me." (See Ephesians 6:18, Romans 8:26.) Then I start praying in tongues. I have no idea what I'm praying or what any groaning of the Spirit communicates, but God does. I know I'm praying a selfless prayer because the Spirit drives it. I'm not getting in the way with my desires.

One night, I had a dynamic prayer session for my future husband. I had no idea who I was praying for, but my prayers started off by praying in the Spirit. I'll share with you a journal entry I wrote about it:

> *Cheryl's Journal (08/27/07)*
> *I had a prayer time that felt like a "tearing down strongholds" prayer. It had a new power behind it. I started*

praying words out loud that felt like receiving a picture and describing its interpretation in story form. I prayed about the angels that had been going to work on the mountain between my husband and me, that we were close. There's now just one mountain in front of us that is tall but not seemingly wide or thick. The angels have chosen a small chisel to work on this wall over time. It seems like with each chip, not much is happening because the barrier remains between us. The angels chisel a line from the bottom to the top, to make a crack in the entire mountain. I could tell once they finish, they'll take their strong arms and shove the two pieces of the mountain apart. The prep time has been chisel time, chipping away at little bits. Upon moving the two pieces apart, we're facing each other, already close because there wasn't a great distance across this mountain. We'll only be standing a few feet apart once the angels move the two pieces of the mountain aside. I haven't felt the power of this type of prayer in a long time. It was neat.

Man of My Dreams (*Eh, hem.* That's God!)

I've mentioned often how God speaks to me through dreams. Over the years, there have been many dreams about my husband and where he was on his journey. God used illustrations that gave me specifics to pray for. Once, God sent me a dream that used the illustration of a pie. It posed the question, "Do you want a pie to be taken out of the oven before it's cooked, or do you want to wait until it's fully cooked and will taste good?" Within the dream, I chose to wait. My future husband was supposedly the chef preparing that luscious pie for me. He wasn't allowed to come out of the kitchen until he was done. It was a cute dream. My friends have often heard me refer to my future husband as "still baking."

In another dream, God used the illustration of my husband as a student. I gathered the last of the materials this man needed for his final classes, but I wasn't the one who was allowed to deliver the materials. Someone else was. In other words, I wasn't to be used as a "teacher" in this man's life.

Every time God's given me a new illustration or new way to pray for this man, it's charged my prayers. Ask God to show you any specifics to pray.

Be Faithful and Not Angry

I learned something about myself that had to change: my tendency to be judgmental. It began in 2004 when God told me He had completed the necessary prep work in me for marriage but that my husband wasn't ready yet.

Don't be judgmental about the lack of readiness of your missing guy. It may have nothing to do with immaturity, flaws, or problems. He may have certain tasks to complete before God wants you together. Maybe he needs to get fully established in his career, finish a degree, or get settled in his home, ministry, or spiritual life. He may need to have these things complete before your wistful beauty can become a royal distraction.

Let the man build a life worthy of inviting you into. Don't rush him—in prayer or in person. It's like trying to let a chick out of an eggshell before it's time. They will not survive because the proper muscles will not be ready. Let him build the right muscles. It's for your own good.

Bottom line: don't prejudge the man. Love him where he's at, even if you don't know where that is. (I must resist the temptation to take out a missing person's report!) If he were supposed to be in your life right now, courting you, he would be. Wait for him.

Hey God! Is He "The One"?

Before leaving this chapter on praying for your husband, I want to address praying about a particular man. Throughout your journey, you are likely to notice certain "suspects." You'll wonder about guys who step into your life or guys who've been in your life that you're now noticing in a new way. This is normal and part of the process. Eventually, we will need an answer from the Lord about whether we should date or consider a particular guy.

I've asked God to weigh in on certain guys. The answer could come from God speaking to me or any of my prayer counselors.

When you feel a "suspect" has stepped into your life, it's important you not race ahead and start filling in your potential story with your mind, with your own pen. (This is so hard not to do!) You can pray *about* him, but it's safest not to pray *for* him to turn out to be "the one."

If you start asking *for* someone, your emotions about that person get muddy. Praying for someone is an emotional act and may cause you to feel things for that person you are not meant to feel, especially if you pray for him as a potential husband candidate. Don't do that to yourself! It will only confuse you further and you may start filling in pages of your version of your love story rather than waiting for God's script.

It's acceptable to pray about a person's life and what he is going through, but don't pray for God to make that person your husband.

When you do finally meet this man and get married, you'll discover all the reasons he couldn't have been in your life until the appointed time. This is a good time to thank God for His perfect timing and humbly admit God was right to make you wait. It's part of your grand story that only God can write.

Assignments:

1. *Keep praying for your future mate.*

2. *Love him enough to pray for him, and to also ask God if there are adjustments God needs to make in you so you'll be prepared to be a wife, including ways you could complement your future mate.*

3. *Keep a journal of all the words you feel God reveals to you during prayer, dreams, visions, and through others. Save these treasures to share with your husband one day. These pieces will ultimately make up your love story.*

CHAPTER ELEVEN

How to Make the Most of Your Life While You Wait

WHY IT'S GREAT TO BE SINGLE:
(An Itemized List of Undisputable Evidence)

1. *I get to make all my own decisions, and I don't have to "call home" to ask if I can go out after work.*
2. *I get to spend all holidays with my family. (In my family, this is a great thing! We enjoy our zany traditions!)*
3. *I get to spend, save, give away, and budget my money the way I want. This includes staying on track with my frugal nature.*
4. *I get to travel when I want.*
5. *I get to go to bed when I want, and there's no one snoring beside me.*
6. *I don't have to spend money on fancy lingerie. (I have to admit, I wish I did!)*
7. *When I want to write, I don't have someone interrupting me or in my space.*
8. *I get to pick my own church and Bible studies that suit my style of worship, prayer, and teaching.*

---

9. *My apartment stays organized and neat, the way I like it.*

10. *I can eat whatever I want for dinner without worrying about someone else's dietary needs and tastes. If I want cereal for dinner, I can have it! I can eat my festive salad with pickles every night of the week and not bother anyone.*

11. *I always know I'm the last person who used my toothbrush.*

12. *I have privacy in the bathroom.*

13. *I get to hang out on my web-cam with my good friends and chat without worrying about someone else eavesdropping.*

14. *I can sporadically shave my legs in the wintertime.*

15. *I don't have children taking up my time, resources, and changing the course and focus of my life.*

16. *I'm not having communication problems, conflicts, and needing to compromise.*

17. *I get to watch what I want on TV, and fall asleep to silly, 80s sitcoms. I have control of the remote.*

18. *I have a lot more time to do whatever I need to do or want to do.*

19. *I'm not caught up in someone else's life problems.*

20. *I get lots of quiet, peaceful alone time.*

21. *I know what position the toilet seat will be in when I sit down in the middle of the night with the lights off.*

22. *I don't need someone's permission to live in Los Angeles and work as a screenwriter.*

I am a very selfish person, aren't I?

I've heard marriage and becoming a parent are sure cures for selfishness—if we let them be. Suddenly, the needs of a family trump our own. That "me focused" list shows how selfish I'm allowed to be, but that's not the point of why I included it here. I don't promote being selfish.

Do you see there are a lot of benefits to be grateful for, during this season of singlehood? I want us to see—with clearly opened eyes— how blessed we are. Those benefits may disappear the moment we're married. Make your own list! You probably have other things you enjoy that you'll have to give up once you're married.

Being single is not an excuse to be selfish. Some of our extra time should be devoted to serving others since we don't have a family to serve in this season. However, there are things about my life I enjoy that I know I will miss once I'm married. I sure want to enjoy them while they are still here! In the same way, once married, I will enjoy benefits only married people should enjoy, but it's a trade-off.

> *Cheryl's Journal (10/01/06)*
>
> *When I was listening to my friend's husband speak at the prayer meeting, I was hearing what some of these changes must feel like to get married. An oddness hit me. An appreciation of where I am because when life changes, it will really change. It's different. It's not bad, but I bet I'll feel a little scared. I need to be ready for this. This change I've been asking for, for so long, when I realize it's about to happen, it might feel overwhelming. I'm so used to things being a certain way, so it will be different. I have to admit: I'm afraid that once it's here, it won't be "all that" and I'll wonder why I spent most of my adult life wanting it to change.*

Some single people—and I've been guilty of this—believe life gets better once you're married. It's not necessarily better; it's different. It brings with it a new wave of benefits and challenges. Some of its challenges come from the loss of benefits you have as a single. It's an adjustment. I have met people who think marriage is the best life change that's ever happened to them. Their conversations usually land on, "What are you waiting for, Cheryl?" Sadly, they are the minority.

A lot of married couples I know have many challenges, often wishing they had the benefits of my single life. They say, "Life was so much easier then." We may think our lives would get better because we'd have the help we need to weather this challenging life, but we forget we're inviting another human being into our hearts and lives. They come to the table with the same amount or more challenges than we already face.

Let's talk about some of the ways we can enjoy this season and what we can focus on—rather than always hoping life would change.

Focus on God and Growing Your Relationship with Him

Spend time in the Word. Get involved at your church or in Bible study groups or prayer groups. Choose ones that will help you grow closer to God, ones that will challenge you in your walk and not encourage you to just stay as you are. Grow your prayer life and your intimacy with Christ. Just like we talked about in the Marriage Boot Camp chapter, we can prepare for marriage as we foster a marital style relationship with God.

How easy is it to become distracted by everything but God? I wrote the following journal entry when I felt like I'd been pursuing avenues to dull my boredom and loneliness:

Cheryl's Journal (10/20/08)
I often speak of feeling invisible to others in my life—namely guys. I often feel overlooked, ignored, not even considered. Is there a parallel here? Does God ever feel that way with me because of the way I sometimes treat Him?
He pursues me; I pursue man.
He waits on me; I reach for comfort food.

He whispers to me, but I turn on the TV.
He wants to talk, but I call a friend.
He wants to walk; I drown my thoughts in music on my MP3.
Temporary pleasures.
Heads turn to the side; the pull is strong. Yet, it's so unsatisfying
after the first few moments or hours. It's dead and empty.
Fulfillment lasts but a fleeting moment. It lacks substance. I need to
keep my head from turning.

Focus on God's Call for Your Life

I realize some of you may not be clear on your calling just yet. You may still be asking what God specifically created you to do. Use this time to seek Him diligently about how He wants to use your life. Does God want you to use this time of freedom to study, to go back to school, to train for your life's purpose?

I've known for a long time that my purpose is to reach people through writing. However, from day to day, I don't necessarily know on which writing project I am to focus. That can change. I often pray, "God, what's today's assignment? Are we mapping out a storyline for a future script? Are we writing a new draft of an old script? Am I writing a chapter of a book today?" God is my best consultant for what to work on because I depend on Him for inspiration. Occasionally, when I choose the wrong assignment, I can tell. The motivation just isn't there.

I love writing and love that God has given me such a fun profession. It's creative, meaningful, and gives me a way to leave my voice, life's message, and impact on people. I don't know how much time I'll have for writing books and movies once my family life begins. I have married writer friends who find it difficult to slip away from everything and spend time at the computer writing their stories, scripts, or books. I realize one day this will be an adjustment. I will have to surrender many of those hours.

What's your purpose? What inspires you most? Have you already trained for it or are you just discovering what God may want you to do with your life? I realize our purpose may change and grow over time, as well. There may not be just one answer to this question. You may also have more than one way in which God will use you. We are all unique; we're called to play a role in God's "Bigger Picture." Don't miss it. Don't spend so much of your time focusing on the search for a husband that you miss the work God has before you right now. God may need to train you for a work you're going to do together with your husband. You just never know. You may not be working in the job you feel is your calling right now, but it, too, prepares you for what's next.

Focus on Assignments God Puts Before You

God always has an assignment, a task, a work for us to complete. Daily. Pay attention. In this case, I'm not talking about the big purposes. I'm talking about the little things in our day-to-day life. It could be the person where you work who doesn't know Jesus. Maybe your assignment is to be that person's friend, to surrender some of that free time you'd rather keep to yourself.

Whether it's tasks or people, ask God for your daily assignments. One of those just might lead you to the right person. I have to admit each time I start a new job or project, I wonder: *Is this it, God? Is this the vehicle You'll use to usher a man into my life?* Well, so far, I haven't seen that happen. You never know. If you resist an assignment, you may be resisting God's way of answering your prayer.

Focus on Blessings You Have in Front of You

We focus on what we don't have—the husband—rather than the wonderful blessings we do have before us. Choosing to not freak out when God allowed me to lose most of my earthly possessions was good practice for that. I believe it was no accident that trial happened when I was writing a movie that's about the gifts in our lives and how they are not possessions or money. Instead, true treasures are people—family and friends. True to the message of *The Ultimate Gift,* sometimes a blessing comes in the form of a problem or a trial. Don't miss seeing these for what they are: they might be graduating you to the next level.

To follow is an angst-filled journal entry that shows how thankless I was for the season God had me in:

Cheryl's Journal (09/05/05)
It's sad to me that in June, I believed my life was changing. I believed I was upon a new season. Well, I was wrong. I always expect the best and life never lives up. The pain of my loneliness is never ending. I am a mess. You are my Father. I need rescuing and care. I can't live in this situation anymore. This has to change, no matter what You have to do. Things can't stay "as is." Why is this the story You're telling? Why is this what You want for me? Why are all of Your choices for me so hard? Where is the promise? The changes? I'll shut up now.

When I started the research for this book, I dug out my old journals to look for entries to use. I was embarrassed by how repetitious my journals were. Year after year, I didn't grow. My prayers didn't change. I spent so much time asking God for the same blessing: my M.I.A. husband. Sometimes, the words were identical, even though written years apart. I wonder if I had just let it go and spent more time enjoying life "as is" if I would have lived those years with less angst. Living with the angst didn't bring about any results. Obviously! I'm still single! (Did I not learn anything from those moan-head Israelites in the desert?) Would I have enjoyed that time more if I hadn't spent so much time dwelling on what I didn't have? Instead, I continuously wrote, "God, do something." "God, change this!" "God, please move me forward." I wish I could have just let it go. I still have to remind myself to do so.

Focus on Activities You Love to Do

If you don't have them, get hobbies! Find something fun and creative to do that you enjoy, something you may not have time to do once you're married with children.

My mother, my sister, and I enjoy scrapbooking. We spend many hours, each time we get together for visits, designing creative scrapbook pages. Of course, my sister's scrapbooks are filled with her two young boys and her husband. My mother mixes it up: some pages star me and my film adventures, others feature my sister's family or our Disney and ski vacations.

Then there are my scrapbooks. Occasionally, it bothers me that I don't have my own family or children to scrapbook. As I work on my pages, I can't deny that I've had a rewarding and fun life, especially once *The Ultimate Gift* happened. I've built many pages of the fun times that movie brought into my life: visiting the set, bringing my family to the red carpet premiere, attending all the award shows and charity events, collecting the newspaper articles and interviews on the film. My other writing jobs supply the same. It's fun to document those blessings. I also enjoy rollerblading, hiking, walking, movies, talking to friends on web-cam. There's a lot we can do for fun that we don't have to wait for a husband to enjoy!

Focus on Serving

How can you serve others? Where can you volunteer your time, resources, and talents? Serve in various ministries where you become a mentor to someone else. Serving doesn't have to be difficult or boring. Choose something that interests you. If you have a talent you're not using, donate it to a church or a nonprofit ministry. Because prayer and encouraging others to hear God's voice are passions of mine, I ran a prayer group for writers for over a year.

Focus on How You Can Turn Your Life Experience into Ministry Opportunities

God has me do this all the time through my writing or through ministering to other people. I have painful experiences that have been used to help other people. My heart for abused kids led me to work with a kid at a group home and at-risk kids at a high school.

My angst as a single person has resulted in many scripts, a novel, and a non-fiction book. I insert myself somewhere in just about every script I write. Whenever I write something that feels honest because it's based on me, I know it's going to resonate with someone who needs to hear it, one who needs to know that someone out there understands.

My battle with a panic disorder is shared in my autobiography — the one I can't publish until I get married. My experience hearing from God through prophetic dreams is in a book and a suspense-thriller screenplay. I love when God shows me how to share my life with others. You can do the same. Make a list of the life issues where you feel you understand pain. Ask God to bring people into your life that you can help who struggle with similar pains. (See 2 Corinthians 1:4.)

Focus on Fulfilling Dreams

What is your dream? What have you always wanted to do? Don't wait to fulfill it until you find a mate. I have a friend who loves to travel, and every year, she takes exotic trips with girlfriends. She's not waiting until she gets married to see the world. If you've always wanted to own a home, work toward it! Don't feel like you need to know where you will live once you get married to invest in your future that way. If you've always wanted to try something, like scuba diving or hang gliding, find a friend with the same dream. Fulfill it together. Follow the passions of your heart, as the Lord allows. God isn't all about pain and suffering. He created laughter and the ability to feel joy. So, live your life to the fullest!

I'm sure there are many other passions you can focus on while you wait. I've just highlighted some here. Make a list! Dare to dream. Go fulfill those dreams or take steps to get closer. Be open to whatever God may lead you to do while you wait.

Plus, you are not just here to wait. You are here to *live*. You're here to do something. Believe me! I have to remind myself of this all the time. I can't tell you how often my Facebook statuses say such lines as, "Cheryl is still waiting" or "Cheryl doesn't think the 'holy pause' is all that holy." Those friends of mine who know what I'm talking about always get a good kick out of it. They know I'm trying to be funny, yet I mean it, too. I just encourage you to make the most of life while you wait. Don't let your life be defined by the word *wait* any longer.

CHAPTER TWELVE

God, the Romancer, Creator of Love

Cheryl's Journal (09/09/07)
Jesus as my Husband will never die. He'll never stop loving me. He'll never leave and not come back. I won't ever have to mourn Him. Jesus, You're the One I will always have with me no matter what comes ahead.

I walked into a prayer meeting in need of a touch from God.

A young woman praying for me said: "God wants you to know that you were named *Cheryl* for a reason. Do you know what it means?" She didn't know me; she didn't know what my name meant. She didn't realize how often in my life I had felt unloved or how what she said touched my heart.

Beloved.

My name means beloved. Here God was, showing up at a prayer meeting, to let me know I was named Cheryl because of that.

That wasn't the first time God used names to reach me. When my last relationship ended painfully, one of the most unintentionally hurtful things the guy I'd been dating said was that I was not a treasure to him. He said he'd prayed God would make me one, but God hadn't done it. This cut to the deepest core of my soul. I believed I wasn't a treasure or worthy of love. After all, no one in my life had ever been in love with me, that I was aware of, so clearly there was something wrong with me, right? God had damage control to do, to perform some serious healing from those painful words.

That's when God gave me an affectionate nickname: Ruby.

It started simply. I'd be at prayer meetings and people would say, "God is calling you Ruby." Or God would send me to a particular place in Scripture that would have the word "ruby" in it. Or I'd go to the store and feel like I should walk over to a particular sign and read it. Sure enough, the word "ruby" was on the sign. I mentioned earlier that I call these moments God Winks.

I accepted each moment like this as God saying "hello." One time, I was sitting on a bench in Santa Monica, teary about how down I felt about my apparent lack of lovability. My cell phone rang; I answered it. The caller asked for "Ruby." I told the guy he had the wrong number. As soon as I hung up, I smiled. Could it be? Could God have directed that wrong number just to say hello? Did He want to remind me that He considers me a treasure, no matter what the opinions of men may be? It was sweet. I welcomed such "interruptions" and reminders about an area that caused me much pain.

Can you think of any moments you'd also call "God Winks"? Think of precious nudges from heaven where it seems God says, "I'm here, and I'm paying attention. I understand your pain."

Cheryl's Journal (01/15/06)
   To Be Known
   I'm tired of having something to say and no one to say it to.
   My writing is my outlet to speak yet I'm silenced with two
   books I can't publish because the person isn't here. I'm silenced

in life because people don't want to know anything. The ache to be known: God experiences this. Do we ask Him questions? Do we dig into who He is? Do we ask His memories? His feelings? Lord, what is Your preferred way for people to get to know You? I can think of a few:

Spend time with You.

Sit at Your feet.

Wait on You.

Ask Your opinion.

Read Your Word.

Know Your story/history.

Pray to You.

Talk to You.

Listen to You.

Obey You.

Follow Your advice.

Follow Your example.

Put You first, make You a real priority.

Give to You.

Give to the least of these.

Get to know Your family members (Jesus, Holy Spirit, our brothers and sisters in Christ).

People say they know You, but do they? Or do they just know of you? Are we afraid to get to know You because we're afraid of what You'll ask of us?

To Dance with God

Have you ever thought about God as a romantic God? There's a reason God equates the return of Christ for the church as a bridegroom returning for His bride. (See Revelation 19, 21, and 22.) God loves romance; He created romance. You can't read Song of Solomon and not find God romantic.

While God may not show up in my living room as a handsome

male my age (as depicted in *Never the Bride*), I believe He is just as involved in our lives as if He were here in the flesh.

One time, when I was frustrated with God, a friend prayed for me and said I needed to find my "dance moment" with God. This was especially meaningful because I'd written a dance scene between God and Jessie in *Never the Bride*. It's a special scene where Jessie's eyes first open to God as Someone worth loving. My friend prayed I'd have that special moment of intimacy with God that wasn't about the norm: the practice of prayer, the practice of reading the Bible. No. *The Dance*. It meant the world to me that God was asking for my hand in a dance.

Have you ever been to a dance and stood on the sidelines with no one to ask you to dance? I have, and it's not fun. To know that God wanted to walk up to me with His hand extended was beautiful.

I feel like God wants to bless me with marriage more than I want it, but He loves me too much to let it happen too soon or with the wrong person. He takes His custody of that pen seriously. He needs me to want what He wants for me, rather than what I want for me.

Are you ready to want what He wants, rather than what you want? It's hard. I have to surrender to this every day, especially because in "Cheryl's will," *today* would be the day.

Our Romantic God

As I pointed out in the beginning, God is a God who sets up love matches. He set the precedent for this in His Word. If you want to read about devoted lovers, read Song of Solomon, or the story of Mary and Joseph.

Let's look at another example, one that involves a second marriage: Ruth and Boaz. Interestingly, this is when God woke up a man to the right woman, yet the woman seemed to know first. I think Ruth's story should be especially inspiring to those who've lost husbands. As a widow, God still had a plan for her life in love, marriage, and motherhood. Ruth walked right into it.

When Ruth made the sacrificial choice to stay with her mother-in-law after the death of her husband, rather than returning to her family, she had no idea what God was up to. She just followed her heart into an amazing act of servanthood.

Once Naomi and Ruth moved back to Naomi's old hometown, Ruth went to work in the fields of a man named Boaz, gathering grain in the field. Boaz noticed her right away; he asked who she was. He met her and set up protective measures by insisting she work only in his field, so he could keep an eye on her. He told all of his workers to leave her alone. Some women who worked in fields like this were taken advantage of by men.

Ruth's heart was simply to serve and take care of her mother-in-law and provide for them. She had no idea of the love story God was writing and how it involved setting up the family line of King David. That same line led to Jesus Christ.

When the right time came, Ruth laid down at Boaz's feet. When he woke up, it was the beginning of him "waking up" to the love story God was weaving: this young woman would become his wife. He didn't immediately try to take advantage of this. He pointed out how she wasn't off chasing after younger men (Ruth 3:10). Her choice and obedience led to her marriage. They built a family together as Ruth bore him Obed, the father of Jesse, who was the father of King David.

This was a God-orchestrated love story that came to Ruth as she was serving someone else. Her motives were pure; she wasn't there to land a husband. It's a blessing God brought to her while she blessed other people.

We can be inspired by Ruth's example. Often, we work hard to make our love stories happen. Maybe—like Ruth—all we need to focus on is loving and serving God and the people He's placed in our paths, and allow Him to line up the right circumstances.

A Love Letter to God

While waiting for your natural husband, take the time to write love letters, poems, and notes to God. I enjoy doing this. It reminds me how much He loves me and is there for me in ways no human can match. I enjoy showering God with the love He so richly deserves for loving the incredibly flawed version of me.

Cheryl's Journal (07/27/06)
    "An Ultimate Love"
    God, the One who loves me.
    Unconditional is His name.
    There is One who loves me.
    Salvation, He bears my shame.
    There is One who loves me.
    He died for every sin.
    There is One who loves me.
    Truth, there's none like Him.
    There is no greater love I could experience than the love of this One.
    This God.
    The devotion of the Son.
    The warm hug of His Spirit.
    He aches when I ache.
    He listens when I cry.
    He accepts my faults.
    Yet, He encourages me to do better.
    To be better, to be like all the best in Him.
    He takes my good and makes it better.
    He takes my worst and covers it with His blood.
    He cleanses me with healing waters.
    He knows the deepest parts of me, unlike any other.
    He listens more than He talks.
    He hears all my cries.
    He sings songs over me when I cry.
    He whispers in my ear when I need encouragement.
    He shows me a verse to brighten my day.
    He whispers a verse for me to give away.

He leads my steps, gives me direction.
He guides.
He counsels.
He heals.
He embraces.
He speaks.
He writes me dreams.
He authors my life purpose.
He directs.
He encourages.
He warns.
He corrects.
He loves me as a daughter. A sister. A bride. A friend.
He loves taking walks with me.
He likes my attention being on Him.
He listens.
He watches over me while I sleep.
He spends time with me.
He considers me His bride.
He makes me feel like His only bride, even if He has many.
He makes promises that He will fulfill.
He winks at me.
He sometimes warns me of bad things to come, out of love for me.
He works with me.
He doesn't leave me alone.
He cares.
He protects and provides.
He knows me, inside out.
He knows my story — He's been there to see all of it.
He likes to sit on my couch at night and hang out.
He loves me unconditionally.
He gives me flowers and sunsets.
He writes love stories like no one else.

God is a romancer. No one can match His love. No one in this world can love me more than Him. None. My search to find a love greater is fruitless. God's love is unmatched. We search for many things to fill our God-sized holes. Only He can fill. Only He can fulfill. Only He can reach.

My Love Example

God gave me a great example when He placed me in my family. My parents, Tom and Denise, are still in love over forty-five years later. I will never forget the day my mom told me the cutest story. She and my father were traveling. They stopped at a rest area, and she stood outside waiting for my dad to come out of the welcome center. As soon as she saw him round the corner, her heart leaped. She thought, *Wow! I still feel that over him!* She was so excited to see him, even though they'd been traveling in the car together for hours and had only been apart a few minutes.

My parents have been an example of love, respect, and devotion, through good and tough times. I've been so blessed to be surrounded by their love and support all these years. They are best friends. I never questioned for a moment whether their marriage would last. Every Valentines Day, my dad gets my mom two dozen roses. In my frugal opinion, one dozen would be plenty. You should hear the pride in my mother's voice as she tells people, "My husband got me two dozen roses." I know he loves to do it!

I don't know what man God has for me. Whoever that man is, I bet he's unbelievably special, and that one day, I'll say the wait was worth it. I can only hope the same for you. Even more so, my prayer for you is that you will accept God's proposal, that you will enter into an intimate, heavenly romance surpassing any love story this world could ever have to offer. Imagine it. The God of the universe has extended His hand in marriage to you, His Bride. He is watching, waiting, longing to hear you finally say, "I do."

CHAPTER THIRTEEN

Are the Dots of My Love Story Finally Connecting?

FACEBOOK STATUS UPDATE:
My sister informed me today that my 5-year-old nephew,
Jake, would like to marry me when he's "growed" up. Gotta
love a little guy with good taste who knows what he wants.

I had hoped this chapter would be named "epilogue" — my last one — and my chance to share the pay-off of my God-written, earthly love story. I guess you could say life *may not* be cooperating. It took me a little over a year to pen this book up through the previous chapter. I wrote all of it while I was still single; I didn't write it after the pain was gone and forgotten. Actually, it's still not gone; it's still not forgotten.

Since I put my pen down after writing the previous chapter, yet another year of my life has gone by. As of now, I remain single. I have been through additional experiences that raised — then dashed — my hopes with men since penning that last page. Since then, I also did many television, radio, and print interviews on the topic of singleness and waiting on God that tied to the book release of *Never the Bride*. It's been an issue that's been in my face constantly, as I try to encourage others to have faith. Yet, there have been days I've had little faith of my own.

I'll never forget the day a new radio show was released eight months after I recorded it, and I hated hearing my own advice. Let's just be honest here, okay? Sometimes, I don't want to live by my own advice and the ways I feel God wants. I have no doubt this book is challenging to take at times for readers—who are no different from me—and still waiting. This topic suddenly becoming my ministry has made the wait that much harder, as I am constantly reminded about my absentee husband and family.

I'm starting this chapter because of a current, deep pain. I don't know what the end of this book will be, how many more chapters it will require, or if it will have the ending I desire. I just know, to be as honest with you as I can be, I need to start this segment while the pain is still fresh in my heart.

I talked about "The Best Friend's Syndrome" in the chapter on the hazards of singlehood. In the friendship I am about to share with you, I didn't follow my own advice outlined in that chapter. I did not withhold emotional intimacy from this person. I might have fallen into the same trap, made the same mistakes I warned you against. There were reasons I broke some of my own rules, reasons why I felt this friendship was different from all the rest. The truth is, I don't know yet if I'm right or wrong. I am paying a high, emotional price.

A Wedding Date

On October 25, 2009, I went to an event where a preacher spoke. He talked to me afterward about relationships and the story of *Never the Bride*; I admitted it was semi-autobiographical. He told me to take out my journal and declared, "By this time next year, you will be married. Write that down!" Believe me! I wrote it down. (I may have been tempted to laminate it, frame it even.) I wanted to believe he was right, that he was being prophetic and not just expressing his hopes for me. I wondered if God would actually give me a timeline.

I went home and prayed about this, for confirmation, and sensed God say to my spirit, "That's the same timeline I gave Abraham and Sarah." I checked Genesis 18, and sure enough, God told them "by this time next year" they would have a son. Remember Abraham and Sarah had to live through almost twenty-five years worth of promises for a child before God gave them a timeline that told their long wait was nearing its end.

My first conversation with God—when He promised I'd get married one day—was over fifteen years ago. So, I have many years of waiting for a promise behind me, too. I took this potential prophecy through the preacher seriously. I say "potential" because I was too afraid to embrace it readily. I feared it had the chance of crushing my spirit if I believed it fully and October 25, 2010, came and went, with no change in my love life.

The night that word came to me, I had a dangling interest that I knew wasn't God's best. I needed to distance myself from him. Honestly, I felt like he equated to the bad distraction my character Jessie had in *Never the Bride* that slowed down the start of her love relationship. I didn't want anything getting in the way of my love story starting. So, just five days after this potential timeline came to me, I told my friend I needed to end our friendship. It was the right choice; I needed to be free of it.

A New Friend

Two weeks later, I was at a prayer fellowship new to me. In fact, it was leaving a particular church I was a part of for three years that drove me to this new fellowship. We were having a party. Across the yard, I spotted a guy who smiled at me. He caught my attention right away. I had never seen him before and wondered who he was. What I didn't know yet is that he had been through a break up just two months prior and also found his way to a new church. A guy who attends his new church happened to invite him to our party. The dots that brought him to the party were not unlike my own.

His name was Dylan.

I ran into him at the end of the party in the driveway, and we talked for about forty-five minutes. I thought he was fun and we clicked immediately. He asked me if I had a Facebook page, and just an hour after the party, I found that he had friend-requested me. Within a week, he bought my book and movie. Some of my friends don't even do that, so he impressed me!

Answer the Call

Dylan and I stayed in touch through Facebook and email for the next six weeks throughout the holidays and travels. Then, the first week of January 2010, I had a dream. I was slightly interested in another guy. I got a dream that seemed to indicate that while that guy was a good person, he was not God's best choice for me. The dream presented a challenge to me: would I let that go and be open to something new God wanted to do? Naturally, when I woke up, my response to the dream was a resounding yes!

Right away, I let go of that other interest in complete peace. That day, I got a strange sense in my spirit that soon, I would receive my first call from Dylan. I sensed I was to pick up the phone, and that his phone number would start with three particular digits. I don't pick up unfamiliar calls, so knowing this information helped. It was one of those weird moments I wondered if I were hearing correctly. Only time would reveal. Sure enough, that same night, the call came in, its first three numbers matching what God seemed to whisper.

We talked for three hours that night. I had to laugh inside when he told me what chapter he was on in *Never the Bride*: Chapter Twelve. Remember what Chapter Twelve means to me? Yeah, it's my nickname for my missing husband.

Naturally, I wondered why God seemed to point him out to me, telling me he'd call and to answer. I knew, historically, with the guys I agreed to date in the past ten years, God told me about them first. Because of my issues with fear and dating, I think God helps me by encouraging me toward particular relationships. Is that what God was doing this time?

Dylan texted me the next morning to let me know he had already finished my book, even though he had 160 pages to go when we hung up at midnight. He couldn't stop reading. He often declared my character Jessie as extremely lovable. Only once I had the guts to pipe up with, "I'll take that as a compliment, considering she's me!" He wanted to set a plan to see each other in person again.

Early on, I started praying for guidance from God about our friendship. One specific prayer I revisited was, "Lord, can you move me out of the second act of my life and finally move me into the third act? You know, where the girl *finally* gets the boy?" I was on a prayer walk and felt like I was to walk to a particular park. It's a place where God has talked to me many times, including through signs or license plates on cars. I joked, "Is there something you want to show me at the park, God?" Upon my arrival, I saw a sign at the park that said "3rd Act." I laughed, snapped a picture of it, of course. I asked, "Is that my answer? Are you confirming that you're *finally* moving me forward after all this time?" That, coupled with the possible date in October, fed my hopes.

A New Support System

My friendship with Dylan grew quickly. In January 2010, when my grandmother was dying, Dylan showed an unusual amount of compassion for my family and me. He was a sweet dose of grace during a painful time, often checking in to see how I was doing, including during my trip back East to see her before she died and during the funeral.

When I visited her in 2008, she was well down the road of dementia. She even introduced me to someone as her niece. Right before I left to head home, she pulled me aside and had the most amazing moment of clarity. She said she had been praying for my future mate. She just knew that whomever he turned out to be would be worth the wait. She felt God knew what he was doing, in taking so long to set this up. I started crying. I couldn't believe she remembered the ache of my heart amid her declining mental state.

I had this sense that this was the last "real" conversation I would ever have with my grandmother. (I turned out to be right.) In that moment, I also knew this meant she would not be alive by the time I got married, even though it was what I'd always wanted. She had shared much of the journey with me regarding my issues with fears of relationships, and I wanted her to see me finally win that battle and get married. In that moment, I had total peace in recognizing she wouldn't be there. I knew God gave me the gift of this wonderful conversation instead.

When I sat at my grandmother's bedside before she died, I held her hand for about three hours, often staring at her beautiful engagement ring. Even though my grandfather had died in the sixties, she was still faithfully wearing it. When she died, I inherited that ring.

Right away, I knew I wanted her precious ring to be my engagement ring. In 2003, it was prophesied that I would have an antique style engagement ring, specifically a grandmother's ring. I had no idea at the time it was referring to my own grandmother's ring and that I'd get it seven years later when she died. Getting her ring feels like a way to allow her to participate when that day finally arrives — when I'm *finally the bride.*

Having my friendship with Dylan kick up during this pivotal time felt significant to me. Once I got back from my trip, Dylan started calling me almost every day for the next few months.

Until that point, he was one of few guys who genuinely cared about my life and what was going on. I guess I got used to many being self-absorbed, taking no interest in getting to know me, or only being friends with me because of my career. He was a refreshing guy who asked questions. A rarity in my world! This may seem amazingly simple, but Dylan won me over simply by asking me each night, "How was your day?" He really wanted to know the answer. He invested himself in my personal and professional life. Maybe that's why I went against my own advice about emotional intimacy before there was an established relationship. I had reasons to feel encouraged by him and to believe this time was different. I thought we were moving toward something potentially wonderful.

Neither one of us could believe how alike we were. It was one of the coolest discoveries with each conversation as we uncovered more common ground. Because of that, we had a great understanding for each other and the best, most honest communication. Once we started sharing our commonalities, I remembered a time it was prophesied how much my husband and I would be alike. I went in search of the journal entry where I recorded the words of someone praying over me:

> Cheryl's Journal (07/07/03)
> You and your husband are a lot alike. You'll like the same things. He will impress upon you and encourage you to be more creative and put more of you in your writing. He's encouraging, boosting, loving, supportive. You'll look a little alike. He's a kid at heart, playful. You will understand each other completely. You will finally be understood. This person will know you, will get you because he's also been through fires and pain and rejection.

Not only did that prophetic word description have the potential to match our commonalities, Dylan became a support system for me. Have you ever had anyone be incredibly supportive of you, so if anything or anyone came against you, they were the first to jump to your defense? He was protective of me, my projects, my writing material. I'll be honest; it felt amazing.

Our friendship grew to be wonderful, yet confusing, because as time went on, he wasn't declaring interest or asking me out on what felt like dates, even though we'd spend time together. I surveyed a few people to ask, "If a guy calls a girl all the time, is he interested?" Everyone thought I was crazy to have to ask. But this is *my* life—so-called romantic interest in me cannot be assumed. I've had too many of these friendships grow into nothing or into the guy letting me know he likes someone else, as if I had never even been considered. Dylan was by far the most attentive guy friend I'd ever had, from consistent calls, texts and emails, time in person, and the one most concerned about my life. Our calls were anywhere from one to three hours, most often before bedtime. It was intimate, sweet, and something I enjoyed tremendously. I loved the way we clicked and thought so much alike.

In all ways except what his attention meant.

The D.T.R.

A couple months in, the topic still hadn't come up. It was time for a D.T.R. You know, the dreaded "define the relationship" talk. I was afraid I was getting attached to him while he was only seeing me as a friend. Again, I found myself in a friendship that had all the emotional benefits of being in a relationship without that romantic commitment. It scared me. What was I investing my heart into?

As is often the case with me, I had to be the one to ask for clarity of where he was coming from. Dylan said he wasn't ready for a relationship yet, as he was still getting over the break up that was fresh two months before I met him. However, he didn't cut me off from hope; he didn't say he would never see me "that way." He promised he wasn't like everyone else in my life who's done that to me in the past. He gave me hope, telling me how much he enjoyed having me in his life. He told me he was still trying to figure out where I fit into his, but he knew for sure his life was better with me in it. That gave me enough hope to not run away from him, but it didn't make it easier. How much should I invest, not knowing the outcome? All relationships are a risk. He was a risk I was willing to take. I did not walk away.

Pressing on in Uncertainty

A friend came to visit my apartment, a place I fully plan to move out of once I'm married. (It's too small for two people.) While we were praying, she said, "You're not going to be living here that much longer." I said, "I believe that, too!" I decided to share with her the story about what the pastor said, that if his "prophecy" were true, I'd get to move out by October. She loved hearing this possible confirmation to what she sensed in her spirit. She's the same person who sensed I had a move coming in my life right before toxic mold ate my last apartment. She was right then; I hoped she was right this time, too. When things like this happened, it only encouraged me to stick it out with Dylan and wait.

I should probably mention that during all this, I noticed an old friend from Charlotte was on Facebook under a mutual friend's list. His name was Chris, and I'd remembered him from my church back there. I hadn't known him well, but he'd been nice enough to help me on video projects when I still lived in North Carolina, so I sent a quick note. After he replied, we started emailing to catch up on life since my move to Los Angeles years prior. I could sense his interest, but wasn't really inclined to consider anything beyond casual exchanges with him. Chris and I didn't appear to have enough in common, especially given his desire to work as a missionary in other countries. Living 3000 miles apart would have made it practically impossible to get to know him. Plus, I was already so focused on Dylan. Even though I didn't see Chris as a real consideration, it did make me stop and question if my interest in Dylan would prevent me from noticing other potential candidates. (Didn't I warn against this in a prior chapter?)

As my friendship with Dylan continued to deepen, I went to God with a question. I said, "God, Dylan is precious. I know you're not taking 'nominations' for my husband, but am I allowed to ask You for him? Is that wrong of me? You can say 'no.' I want to put him at Your feet and ask You for him."

Two days later, I was in a prophetic prayer meeting with people who did not know me or anything I was praying for. One lady said, "Maybe you don't feel right about asking the Lord for certain things. The Lord wants you to ask. 'Everything that you ask, I hear so clearly,' the Lord says, 'I won't deny anything, I won't hold anything back.' The Lord wants to encourage you and says, 'Ask Me, ask Me. I long to give that to you. So ask Me.'"

I walked out of that prayer meeting, asking, "You long to give that to me? What I've been afraid to ask You for? Did You just answer my question from two days ago? Are You encouraging me to ask You for Dylan *and* confirming it's the right thing to ask for?" I was happy about that possibility.

A few more weeks went by. I started to doubt God spoke. An opportunity to visit my family in Charlotte presented itself. Chris was enthused to hear about it. He said he wanted to hang out with me, if I were able to get there. After I prayed about the trip, I had a dream that seemed to indicate that if I went to Charlotte, I would undermine the foundation that had been started with Dylan and me. It would derail our relationship. It was still delicate. So, without even telling Dylan I had that decision to make, I chose not to go.

As the time for the trip came and went, I still questioned if my decision to stay for the sake of Dylan was the right one. I didn't know if that was a dream "sent from God" or just a dream where my subconscious was working through its issues. Hearing God's voice is not an exact science. I'm not afraid to admit that amid these "alleged" confirmations, I feared I was crazy or hearing wrong or that the enemy was actively trying to deceive me. The enemy knows the ways in which I listen and hear. Was he using some of God's own kids to participate unwittingly? Can the enemy do that? Those who prayed or prophesied over me were strong believers.

It was so hard to discern. Reality just wasn't matching up. Dylan wasn't asking me out. He wasn't ready or making a move, but he was continuing to call and be a daily part of my life.

A month after the first "Ask Me" prophecy, I went to another

Christian gathering and was prayed over by a different set of people. You can imagine my jaw dropping when someone else who's never met me said God wanted to say to me, "Ask Me, ask Me, and I will give it to you."

You would think if I didn't get the point the first time, I'd embrace it the second. Honestly, it was still hard. I wanted to believe I was just waiting for Dylan to heal then hear God's voice about me, that I was not being deceived. As I said in the "Foreshadowing" chapter, knowing too much in advance can be dangerous! When is it acceptable to believe it? Had I filled in any of the wrong blanks? Had I jumped to erroneous conclusions? I wished I could just believe and wait in peace.

Was any of this real or just coincidences? Coincidence #1: the dual prophetic words about "asking God" after I had prayed if it was okay to ask specifically for Dylan. Coincidence #2: Seeing the "3rd Act" sign right as I prayed about this man. Coincidence #3: Knowing Dylan's number before he called, and many others. Was it enough? Did God have anything to do with this, and if not, why wasn't He stepping in to correct me?

To make matters more complicated, Chris called me and asked if I would consider a relationship with him. While I much appreciated and respected Chris's directness and that he was *actually* pursuing me, I had to say no to him. Given my strong—and growing—feelings for Dylan, I didn't have a choice.

Pulling Away

Life got too painful. As much fun and joy as Dylan brought to my life, I felt like he had gotten too comfortable with our friendship "as is." It seemed like he could have kept things the way they were for a long time. Leading us toward a relationship seemed far from his plans, even though he wasn't interested in anyone else or talking to anyone in his entire circle of friends and family more than he was to me. Honestly, as much as we talked to each other, neither one of us had the time!

By this point, two months had gone by since the D.T.R. It had been six months since we met. We had grown closer, but I felt like I was alone in growing toward love. When I feared that would never happen in him, I had to make the painful decision to take an indefinite break from our friendship. I wanted to "leave" before I fell in love with him. I had only loved one other person in my whole life — the guy I thought I would marry in 2003.

My last phone call with Dylan was three hours long. (Kind of like a bookend, eh?) He didn't want me to cut him out of my life, but I didn't know what else to do. I knew each encounter, each phone call was only investing my heart deeper into him. I made it clear he was only allowed to break the silence and call me if and when he came to a decision about us. Once that was established, we both had a difficult time ending the call. We hung out for another hour on the phone, during which time he continued to share his favorite things about me. I said, "I don't understand you, Dylan. How can you say all that about me and have it still not translate into anything more than friendship?" He had no answer for me. After much stalling, around one o'clock in the morning, we had to hit END CALL. It was the emptiest feeling.

I wondered why reality wasn't matching any of the so-called prophetic words. Where was God in the midst of my shattered heart?

CHAPTER FOURTEEN
Another Heartbreak?

FACEBOOK STATUS UPDATE:
I've decided that the holy repeat is much worse
than the holy pause.

I have felt a great deal of pain since my friendship with Dylan had to go on hiatus. It has been different from when my last relationship ended in 2003. I haven't been angry with God this time. I've been perplexed and asked, "Was this really what You wanted for me? Again? Are we stuck on a divine repeat button or something?" It's still been different. Better. I haven't been oppressed with depression, but I've been grieving.

Sadly, upon taking the break from our friendship, I realized I "left" too late. I had to face the fact that I was already in love with Dylan. He's only the second person I've ever loved that way. I figured it out a few weeks after I cut off communication when I couldn't stop crying over this break. Letting down my walls enough to love someone does not come easily to me. I want him to be the last person I need to do that with. I want it to matter that I love him. I want the chance to enjoy it.

I haven't yet.

On a Mission with God

Right after the initial break, I decided to take a retreat out of town by myself to a mission that had dorms to rent for private, spiritual retreats. It was a special time away with God. I needed it; my soul needed it, but it was painful. God showed up with many winks and treasures. He met me where I was when I went to seek Him fully.

For example, upon arriving at the center, I prayed for God to have the lady check me in to Room Twelve because of my symbolism of "Chapter Twelve." When I walked in the rental office, the lady moved her hand down the chart of room numbers and said, "I'm going to put you in Room Twelve." I laughed, thinking, *Of course you are!* We were off to a great start. It was a sweet, affectionate moment where God seemed to say, "I know where you are. I heard your prayer."

Then I found myself walking into the mission church, which was the original setting of Jessie's church break-in scene in *Never the Bride*, where she dropped off her purple pen at the altar. When I started to walk down the aisle, I laughed. I felt like I stepped into that scene. I was in there by myself (thankfully) and asked God if He wanted me to leave Him my purple pen. (Yes, I had a purple pen with me.) I marched to the front, giggling, and found a place to hide the pen. I didn't want it to get discovered immediately. I wanted it to sit on the altar for a while. I left it behind, laughing at my Jessie moment as I left the church. The next day, the pen was still there. The last day of my retreat, I prayed, "God, it would be neat if the pen were gone. I don't need it to do the writing. You do." Indeed, when I walked up the aisle for that final time, my pen was gone.

I also enjoyed alone time in a chapel with a piano, singing and praising God. There's something about being able to sing and not worry about being heard. I was the only retreat guest at the center that week. I also could dance around the room. I realized I was having my "dance with God" moment and was enjoying His presence in solitude. Just me and Him! No one else.

On the retreat, I had the chance to go to the beach with God alone, something Jessie also does in *Never the Bride*. (No, I didn't tackle Him to the sand to try to steal the purple pen back like she does.) I did, however, just so happen to land at a pier that had a restaurant at the end called Ruby's Diner. I ate there, on the second floor, which overlooked the water and enjoyed my "date with God" alone. (Another scene right out of my script and novel!) It was a precious time.

Perhaps the most specific conversation I felt I had with God was my first night in the dorm. They only had one sitting room called the D room. There was no A, B, or C. Just D. I sat in the room and joked with God, "Come on! Seriously! Why is this the D room? I often call Dylan "D" in journals for the sake of privacy. Then I felt God say, "Go look at the plaque on the door!" Imagine my surprise when I realized the plaque on the D room door said "Gift of Dylan." "Gift of God" is a huge symbol for Jessie's husband in *Never the Bride*. Then I felt like God said I should look at the first letters of each word to see what it spelled. I said, "G.O.D. God. Gift of God. Wow. Really?"

Next, I wanted to ask God about a dream I had about Dylan that morning, right before I left for this retreat. It was a dream where Dylan came up to me and handed me a DVD, said it was his life story and asked me to watch it. It was like watching a flashback of a speech he gave at someone else's wedding, which revealed his heart and who he is and how he views marriage and relationships.

So after God showed me the "Gift of Dylan" sign—which made me wonder if God was winking at me big time by telling me Dylan is my Gift of God—I asked about the dream and what it meant. I felt God ask me, "Don't you think I would preserve something so good for you?" I was afraid to say yes; I wanted to say yes. Being 38 years old, it had gotten hard to believe God had anything in mind for me. I'd been rejected so many times, even by Dylan himself who was the closest to me of almost any guy I've ever known. Yet, I still wasn't enough for him to say yes to.

I told God I wanted to believe and sensed Him say, "This Father only wants to give good gifts to His daughter. Read Verse 11." I replied, "Verse 11 of what?" Then the thought "Sermon on the Mount" came to me. I felt like the verse would be in the "ask, seek, knock" part of Matthew 7 since "ask me" had become a symbol in this story. I read Matthew 7:7-11, and indeed, the eleventh verse was the verse God was referring to:

> "Ask and it will be given to you; seek and you will find; knock and the door will be opened to you. For everyone who asks receives; the one who seeks finds; and to the one who knocks, the door will be opened. Which of you, if your son asks for bread, will give him a stone? Or if he asks for a fish, will give him a snake? **If you, then, though you are evil, know how to give good gifts to your children, how much more will your Father in heaven give good gifts to those who ask him!**"

I wanted to believe God was having a real conversation with me. If all I heard when I prayed was, "You will marry Dylan," I would have tossed it out as my own thoughts. Instead, these questions *seemingly* from God had payoffs I couldn't have predicted or made up on my own. The verse number matching the words. The words and his name on the door. The acronym for Gift of Dylan. I can't make that stuff up myself.

I wanted to believe God was helping me be peaceful with the wait, to trust Him, and to believe He was confirming things would eventually come together with Dylan, that I just had to wait and trust. I was so afraid to believe. I didn't want to hope in vain. I couldn't figure out if I were to process mourning the loss of him or just move my heart back over to "wait mode" for Dylan to get healed and ready for me.

Back to Reality

On May 14, 2010, my retreat ended. Coming home was tough. The retreat was an escape, a precious time of communing with God. Coming home held all the same problems and pains that existed when I left. I was also coming home to a time when I had two bridal showers to attend and a wedding. As some of you may have experienced, those are tough events for a person with a tender and broken heart.

A few days after I returned, we hit the twelfth day since our last phone call. That's the day Dylan chose to break our silence, peeking out over Facebook. He sent an email the next day. Because he had expressed a hope I was doing okay in his note, I used my reply as a chance to tell him I was not, that the break was hard on me. His response was that he had really missed having me in his life and all the joy I brought to him, and he missed the ways I made his life better. While this was great to hear, it didn't help because he still wasn't doing anything that could bring us back together. I couldn't understand why—if he missed me so much—he couldn't see the solution right in front of him. He didn't have to lose me, but he still wasn't making a move. I also have to recognize it's a big decision for him. He couldn't take choosing me lightly, as I'm very much on the marriage track and not just dating casually.

So, I had to keep him at arm's length. In one of his notes, he expressed that he wished I'd come to a party of his. (Staying away just about killed me!) I still felt like I was mourning, much like after a break up, despite any hope God seemed to offer. While we may not have had a physical dating relationship, we certainly had an emotional one, whether we called it that or not. Losing him has been a great loss. He really was—and is—a wonderful guy. I know it was my choice to send him away, at least for now. However, I was too afraid that one day, when he healed from his break up, he wouldn't turn in my direction.

Despite how awesome parts of our friendship were, I have to say there was always this cloud of disappointment or "hope deferred" following it. It was never going to feel like enough until true interest was declared and a relationship was allowed to start. That's why I feel like these friendships can be so unintentionally damaging to the one who is interested while the other isn't there yet. That can happen in both directions. I know guys who find themselves in this painful position with other girls.

Honestly, even as I type this chapter, I still hope it will turn around. As of this writing, Dylan has left town. My prayer has been that he'll seek God while he's gone and have a chance to heal and breathe and then make a choice.

I stand waiting, trying to be obedient to what I feel God wants of me. I don't know if this is going to turn out the way I strongly believe it should.

Before Dylan left town, he wrote to say good-bye. He made it clear he misses me more than he could have imagined. I can only hope, ultimately, that is going to mean something to him. To us. Right now, I don't know. So, I live with the pain of again not being chosen, even by someone who adores me as much as he does.

The pain is still raw. I feel like my right arm is missing. My heart pangs every time the ten p.m. hour shows up on my phone and it doesn't ring because it cannot. I put up the boundary. I hope by the time I end this book I will have a happy ending, with Dylan, to tell you. As of today I wait in hope; I wait in pain.

Someone Else's God-Written Love Story

I went to a wedding of a God-written love story right after Dylan left town. There was a seat ready for him, but I was never able to invite him because of the circumstances. The bride was one of my best friends, Sheri.

When she read my book *Never the Bride*, she had a few random guys in her life that we didn't feel right about. Meanwhile, she'd met a guy at her sister's birthday party named Matthew. I joked, "He should be your guy. His name means 'Gift of God.'" (How right I would turn out to be!) Right after she finished my book, she prayed for a God-written love story and surrendered those wrong guys.

A day later, she got a Facebook friend request from Matthew. (Did you hear me? *A day later*.) On their first date, he told her he wanted God in charge of their story. Yes, he even used "my" terminology from my book without having heard of it. Naturally, Sheri liked his style!

Their courtship began. It took God a whole day to answer her prayer. Of course, she didn't know that right away. They had to walk through a relationship first. One thing she said right away was, "I think God put me in Matthew's heart." It's obvious she was right. He loves and adores her to pieces. They indeed share a God-ordained, God-written love story that He blessed them with so shortly after her prayer. She even got to have purple bridesmaids dresses at her wedding, which has always been my dream. Jessie does this in *Never the Bride*.

They are a good example of how it's supposed to be. A man should lead. A man should submit to God. A man should love and adore his woman. If we find ourselves dating guys where these things are not present, we are not likely in a God-written love story. We still have a chance to get out of it. I want the best for all of us. I'd rather us all wait to find what Matthew and Sheri have found.

I'll be honest. Watching God answer the prayers of a friend, so quickly after reading my book and its message, was a little tough for me. I felt like it worked for her and not me. Sheri's almost twelve years younger than I am. I didn't want anything less for her! She's beautiful, wonderful, and one of the most kindhearted girls I know. I just didn't—actually *don't*—understand why God continues to withhold from me. When she said God put her inside Matthew's heart, it hurt. God can do that, and yet He still hasn't with Dylan or anyone else. It's been a continuing journey to walk through. God doesn't seem to think I need an answer to what He's doing or why He chooses pain for me instead of love.

Some people would say, "Your problem is you put your hope in a particular person instead of God. You wouldn't get hurt if all your hope was in God instead." Honestly, I think we'd have to be emotional robots to do that. Who goes on a job interview, when they need a job, and doesn't hope they get it? Who tries to get pregnant and doesn't hope a few weeks down the road to find out there's a little one growing inside? Who meets a special man when they've been single their whole lives and doesn't hope for possibilities beyond friendship? Hope is an everyday part of life. When allegedly prophetic words seem to be pointing in a particular direction, how are we supposed to shut off hope for them to come to pass?

Ironically, even in the midst of the showers for the bride, God seemed to try to encourage me by reminding me of promises to come. At one of them, the maid of honor had a fun water gun fight planned. They told us we could take home our water guns, so naturally, I saved myself a purple one. I had this thought that there's not much use for one gun, since you need two for a water gun fight. When I was leaving, the bride-to-be asked me if I wanted one of the extra ones someone forgot to take home. I gladly accepted. As I was leaving, I had this sudden memory of a word of prophecy someone gave me in 2004. I looked it up when I got home to see what it said.

> *Cheryl's Journal (05/27/04)*
> *There will be water gun fights around your home. He'll start the chase. There will be lots of giggling in your household.*

I joked with God, "Did you just use someone else's bridal shower to provide the props to fulfill that prophecy about my future love life?" You can bet I'm going to save those water guns, in faith that God meant that prophecy and every other one!

Incidentally, at the shower, I came in second in the "Pin the Bride on the Groom" contest.

(Don't ask!)

A Wedding Plan

It's tough to walk through this journey where there have been so many reasons to hope without a payoff. Over the course of the past year, there's been a lining up of many elements toward a wedding:

I had the engagement ring from my grandmother.

I had the potential "date" by which the wedding would happen. My dad revealed to me that on Valentines Day 2010, while praying for me, he got a strong sense that by Valentines Day 2011, I would no longer be alone. Naturally, I thought the October 2010 wedding date would take care of that one.

I had someone tell me she'd read *Never the Bride,* and God told her to tell me she'd do all my flower arrangements free. I'd just have to buy supplies, but she'd take care of the designs.

It seems like elements are coming together. Except the groom. Oddly, that is the exact storyline of the first romantic comedy I wrote, *Ask Riley,* where my heroine is planning her wedding when she has no idea who the groom is supposed to be.

As of completing this chapter, I have no idea what's going to happen. You're on the journey with me. It's an unpredictable ride. Most people in my life agree this story isn't over yet. It needs its ending, one way or the other.

CHAPTER FIFTEEN

The End or the Beginning...

MISSING:

My husband? No. He's not missing. He's around and just not totally revealed. God knit him in his mother's womb at just the right moment.
Meanwhile, I'm placing this ad to make sure God knows that I love Him as my One True Husband. You, my dear Lord, are all I need. For today.
Please don't change my life one day too soon.

As I open this chapter, it's October 2010. I can say with certainty I am not getting married at the end of this month, but I've known and came to accept it a while ago even though once Dylan came back to town our friendship resumed. It resumed in a more balanced way, no longer conducted like having a relationship without calling it one. Doing this didn't help my feelings go away. Our history made it too late for that. In case you were wondering, he still wasn't asking me out.

When he first returned and had nothing to say about if he was ready for me yet or if we had any future, I was about to walk away again. One of the only reasons I tried to stick it out is that within twenty-four hours of seeing him for the first time since our break, three huge "signs" seemed to smack me in the face. One was a car that's plates were personalized with his initials followed by mine with a giant heart in the middle. I thought it was God's way of encouraging me to wait.

It was not.

After so many of these crazy signs and wonders continued, I finally asked God, "If this is You speaking, could You please stop?" I added that the only sign I would accept was out of Dylan's mouth, saying that he wanted me. No more of this "in the spirit realm," so-far-removed-from-reality stuff. It's not that I was losing faith. I started to wonder if I were actively being deceived by an enemy that would love nothing more than to derail my ministry, pull me away from God, and cause me to mistrust the One who is most trustworthy. The fact that the signs brought anxiety and confusion, not peace, made me wonder if God was truly in it.

He was not.

Honestly, the signs immediately stopped once I uttered that prayer! Maybe something in my prayer kicked the lying devil to the curb. Because there had been so many before that moment, the absence of them was loud.

So, I told you the whole story as it happened. Like me, you may have gotten sucked in for the ride and hoped it would turn out "okay" by my definition. I wrote it while it was happening on purpose, so it could be a divinely written love story if it came to be, or a cautionary tale of mistakes I made if it didn't.

In the bigger picture of my life, everything is okay. This part of my story did not resolve as I had hoped, and as I thought God revealed it would. Nothing ever changed with Dylan. When it came time to bring this situation to a conclusion, I will say it was peaceful and enormously respectful. I still think the world of him, even if I need him to remain at a distance. Thankfully, we were able to be honest with each other about all that had transpired in our hearts and minds throughout our friendship. To respect our privacy, I'm not going to share about that conversation. I did feel a lot better, hearing what he had to say about everything. It resulted in a very amicable ending.

That end helps direct my path forward and yet also away from him—for my own sake and the sake of any future relationships. I have to say my friendship with him was great practice in honesty and sharing feelings in a candid way. So, in that way, I can look at my friendship with him as good preparation for my future.

I learned a lot from the mistakes I made, and I'm happy to share them with you. I strongly suspect that one day I will be happy it fell apart. God knows best what I need, what Dylan needs, and what my future husband needs—whoever he may be. I'm glad Dylan was a praying person. If we were to be together, God would have told him so. I'm glad he submitted to that, rather than us getting into the wrong relationship, only to have to end it. That doesn't mean it wasn't hard to accept at first.

A Crisis of Faith

Before Dylan and I had that final talk and I lost hope of things changing with him, I naturally went through a season of asking God why He let this happen to me. Why, if God seemed to be talking to me about this man, did it all lead into nothing? I asked this question for a couple of months leading up to my end with Dylan, seemingly to no answer, even though I explained to God my question was not rhetorical. I wrestled with what all this meant regarding my own relationship with God. If He hadn't been talking to me about this man this whole time, who was? I was one of God's cheerleaders, telling others they can hear God's voice and have a close relationship with Him. How could I continue to do that if I didn't have a relationship with Him where I could recognize His voice? Talk about a crisis of faith, when faith had always been one of my strongest spiritual gifts.

You can imagine the wide range of doubt and emotions that came with this, right? I put God in a box for a couple months and said I didn't want to talk to Him because I didn't trust Him and His voice. I couldn't talk to a Being who didn't want to have a communicative relationship with me. Right or wrong (I'm thinking wrong), it's what happened, and I took a break from God. It was almost like I wanted God to prove He was talking the whole time—by fulfilling this story with Dylan—to prove I had the relationship with God that I thought I had.

That day never came.

When I started to suspect all those signs were false, I was sadder about what it said about my relationship with God than what it meant about my lack of a future with Dylan. I had to face the question: did I want a relationship with God? Did I want reconciliation, even though I felt so disappointed about many things related to God? Did I want to let this debacle harm my relationship with God and my ministry forever?

Heck no!

As lovely as this guy was, no guy is worth unraveling all that matters in life. I just had to deal with how I felt about all this, be honest with God, release this guy from my life, and then be willing to leave it behind and march forward. Naturally, I needed God's help to do that.

I found peace with it in stages. One turning point was talking to another girl who went through a similar situation but ultimately married someone else. She had a guy behave like a pursuer who wasn't truly pursuing her. She also, like me, felt God led her straight to that guy. This went on for two years. In her case, her guy didn't want to take responsibility for the feelings his behavior encouraged in her, as though she should have known all along his attention didn't mean anything outside friendship. Thankfully, a real pursuer showed up after that friendship ended. She got to feel the difference of what it's like when a guy enters your life who has the capacity to love you.

When I was on a trip, I went with a friend to visit her church. The preacher said, "If you have God in a box, you will never move on to the next chapter of your life." Changing the chapter had huge symbolic meaning to me, as you well know. I wanted to move on, so I could finally enter the marital season of my life. I took that warning to heart.

Once I let it all go, I told God it was okay if I never got an answer to why He let all that erroneous prophecy encourage me along the way. Remember, most of my examples were words from other people or things that happened outside myself I couldn't control. For example, I did not seek out getting someone to prophesy over me that I'd get married within one year.

One of my biggest points of contention with God during this whole saga was that I left town to be alone with God and He still let me be so deceived at the retreat center. I thought, if God can't meet me on a retreat with any degree of authenticity, then what kind of relationship do I have? About the time I surrendered my so-called right to understand, God gave me understanding.

A Truth Revealed

I heard a great sermon where the pastor shared that when you are doing what you're called to do, you may have transition times in the wilderness. While there, we need to press into God in our prayer times. We have to remember, even Jesus, when He went off to pray before He fulfilled God's plan for His life, had to face another voice. He may have gone to spend time with His Father in prayer, but He had to face the devil's voice. We, too, in our prayer times, have to face several voices: our own, God's, and the enemy's. We need discernment to figure out who's who.

The pastor also pointed out that the devil tries to hit you at your area of deepest hunger. Satan appealed to Jesus regarding power and His physical hunger. After the preacher mentioned all that, I was hit with a sudden parallel for what might have happened to me.

As mentioned, I was heartbroken about how I could leave town to be with God and be met with such deception. Is this any different from

Satan showing up during Jesus' prayer time? Jesus is much better at discernment that I am. Satan knows my hearing methods with God; he can certainly counterfeit them. Satan knows my areas of deepest hunger and came after me full force. God's presence was there for my retreat, and nothing takes away from the preciousness of those moments, but I also believe another voice entered to deceive that first night in the dorm.

At least I know I wasn't crazy; I wasn't making it all up. An enemy was at work to derail me, my relationship with God, and my ministry. Gratefully, I usually write about these things to help others, rather than cursing God for allowing me to continue to go through so much pain. (Take that, Satan!)

I've heard many more stories of women who've been through the same thing—not only with guys who might be misleading with their relationship intentions, but also with feeling like God was leading them toward a particular guy. I thought I should include this story as a cautionary tale of how off we can be and how specifically we can be misled. Satan would love for me to lose my faith, curse God, to claim loudly that the story of God and Jessie in *Never the Bride* is a lie. He wanted me to adopt the belief that God doesn't care about our love lives. I'll be honest—it's embarrassing to share this story publicly because it exposes so much of my own error. Because this happens so often to women, especially in church communities, I thought it was worth getting past my embarrassment to share.

I'll remind you of the two most important things this hard lesson has shown me. One, do not give away these kinds of friendships to men without a commitment and clear sense of where your relationship is going. Two, do not trust signs and wonders that point to a particular man as your future spouse. Even in the face of confirmations, when it speaks to your area of deepest desire, there is too much room for error. There's such a high emotional price for this error. I'm not saying God will never speak about these things. Whatever you think you hear may just need to be written down and put away to be celebrated and shared after the fulfillment, if you turn out to be correct. You might need to wait for reality to show you if a prophecy is true or not in this most delicate area of life. I'm sure it happens to men and women alike. Perhaps like Jesus' mother, Mary, said about the prophecy she received, these things are best held close to our hearts and not to be shared unless — or until — the prophecy is proven true.

This might sound funny, but as much pain as that "wedding date" caused me, I was glad to have an expiration date. Having a date that could come and go without the prophecy being fulfilled gave me a chance to let it all go. I know too many women who held onto hope for a particular man far too long after they should have given up, letting new opportunities pass them by. I felt I could tie that wedding timeline with the rest of the prophecies because I met Dylan a few weeks later and everything unfolded from there. He was my only interest as the "expiration date" neared. Once I came to accept those words were off, I was able to walk away from it clean. (By the way, his name is not actually Dylan.)

Do You have a Dude who Hasn't "Woken Up"?

I want to share what I learned with regard to men being pursuers. I started to question what I've heard from many women who feel like God revealed who they are going to marry, but the man doesn't know yet. I witness these stories all the time, but I don't personally know of any that have turned out well yet. I'm sure some have. You may know people who have that story. I've watched women wait years for the guy who is never going to "wake up."

In looking at this trend, I've pondered the character of God. He seems to have called men to be leaders and pursuers. If that were true, would God allow the woman to be the only one who knows the truth about their future for a long period of time? Why should the woman be the only one who can hear God's voice about such an important issue? I've seen marriages where the guy knew first or both spouses heard simultaneously from God. I can't say that I have good examples where the woman knew first for an extended period of time and it turned out well. It doesn't mean it can't or hasn't happened. I read one example in a Christian book. Maybe there's a small element in Ruth laying at Boaz's feet in the Bible. I would never say God can't lead this way. If He did, I'm sure He'd have a great reason for it. He can do what He wants; He's God. I just know many bad examples that have led to years of pain for the women who believe they are in this situation and still waiting for the guy to hear from God.

A New Possibility

I mentioned there being the other man from Charlotte, Chris, who was trying to pursue me. Unfortunate timing for him, I had just fallen in love with Dylan. Add to it the confusion of having the dream that I thought said to stick with Dylan and not take that trip to Charlotte. Now that I know that's not accurate, I can kick out that dream as my own subconscious working through its issues. Even though I said no, Chris did not give up on me. He patiently built our friendship from afar, despite little encouragement from me that there would be any future. In fact, I flat out said "I'm not going to give you any hope for a future with us."

A little history is in order here. Chris and I were friends from the church singles group before I moved to California. I recall thinking of him as "the only cute guy in singles group." As mentioned, Chris helped me on some of my video projects in Charlotte. My sister always wanted me to go out with him. I told her, even though he was quite handsome, I was California-bound. I didn't need anything—or anyone—standing in my way, keeping me on the east coast. I was still in my twenties and had other priorities in mind. Plus, he wasn't asking me out. Though I do remember the first time I saw him with a new girlfriend back then, shortly before I moved. I felt that pang of regret that he'd found someone. That was that. I moved away eleven years ago and haven't seen him since.

We reconnected on Facebook shortly before Easter 2010, about four months into my friendship with Dylan. Naturally, my heart was somewhere else. Over the course of the next six months, despite my "no's," he said he couldn't get me out of his mind as a good potential choice for him.

I knew I needed to heal from Dylan first, but I agreed to get to know him better during my Thanksgiving trip. I did so even with a bit of excitement that couldn't have come until I was willing to let go of Dylan. As of this writing, that trip is one month away. Your guess is as good as mine as to whether it will work out.

Never the Bride: A Prophetic Novel?

Leading up to this trip, I have been captivated by the parallels between *Never the Bride* and the story of my real life. I'm starting to see that, while all the prophecies in my life leading into the situation with Dylan were off base, it's possible God led me to write a prophetic story in my script and novel. I might have been walking through that story—both for Jessie's good moments and her mistakes—unwittingly. The parallels of the novel and screenplay story cannot be missed.

My crisis of faith was exactly like Jessie's, when she tells God that of all those she's ever loved, God has led her on the most. She felt like God was answering her prayers and leading her to one particular man, only to find out God wasn't doing that at all. She questions her sanity and begins to wonder if God was ever there or if she had fabricated His active presence in her life. The parallels to what happened in my life after I wrote that story are remarkable. I had all the same questions, all the same doubts, over an identical situation.

It's also possible that what God was doing has remarkable parallels as well. It means this whole time, God was doing His work "behind-the-scenes" and I was not meant to see it too soon. Funny how often I talked about that being how God works on radio shows, interviews, and at book clubs, yet somehow I missed this in my own story. God gives Jessie absolutely no hints in advance, none of those signs and so-called wonders like I paid attention to with Dylan.

Instead, God wanted her obedience and faith while leaving her in the dark. Also in the story, God gave her the person—over and over again—and she kept rejecting him. Sound familiar? Time will tell if this all tracks with my real life.

In fairness to the pastor who prophesied when I would be married, I couldn't help but wonder. If I had cooperated from the beginning—back in May when Chris first asked me to consider a relationship—could all of this have unfolded sooner? The guy in Jessie's story shows up many times before she finally embraces him. So, in this real life story, I've found myself saying words to God just like Jessie did: "It does not escape my notice that this could have happened a lot sooner if I had cooperated."

Just like Jessie's guy in *Never the Bride*, Chris didn't give up on me. Also like in the story, Chris had to put up with my interest being in someone else. He had to wait for me to give up the other person, "the best friend," to give us a chance.

Another parallel is that when Jessie finally cooperates and gives up the other guy, all God gives her is an address for the guy and says, "Go to him." Now I find myself in a position where I am to go home for Thanksgiving, where this guy also lives, to give "us" a chance. It reminds me of the story of Isaac and Rebekah when she says, "I will go," even though she had no idea what she'd be walking into. It's still a faith walk. I still don't know what the outcome of this story is going to be. Perhaps I'm finally cooperating so life can move forward.

Giving up Dylan was extremely painful for me, but it's a necessary step for this new relationship to have a chance. I even told Dylan that I had the feeling God was trying to bless me this whole time with Chris, but I had been too stubborn to see it.

If you have a male best friend, you may want to consider if that friendship is getting in the way of the right guy being able to capture your heart. It's not that these guys are "bad." It's that these friendships can get in the way of the marriage you desire.

Recently, Chris said to me that he really wanted this situation to not be a Cheryl-thing or a Chris-thing but a God-driven thing. This was before he ordered a copy of my novel. It reminded me of my friend Sheri's beginning with Matthew, when Matthew said the same thing to her about their love story. I respected Chris's leadership in saying that, because that's all I've ever wanted—a man who would choose to be led by God above himself.

For the first time in my life—with Chris—I feel like God is trying to convince me of something, rather than me trying to convince God that I know what and who is best for my life. It's quite a reversal, and *way* out of my comfort zone. God bless Chris for being so patient with me, as I have been so uncooperative.

As ready as I have continuously claimed to be, I have found myself saying "slow down" and "I'm not quite ready for you yet." I never thought "slow down" would come out of my mouth about the love story area of life, when I've historically said (ad nauseum), "Hurry up and move, God!" Naturally, I can't help that I fell in love with another guy and genuinely needed some time to breathe and heal over that one. Chris understands that. In fact, all of his responses to me in this situation impressed me and gave me much peace about giving him a chance.

Onward

I'm happy to say the October 25, 2010 date came and went without incident. It's a testament to the grace God is giving me in the face of disappointment and the ongoing "hope deferred."

Remember I mentioned the sermon that turned my head around in this situation and gave me understanding about how the enemy will speak to our area of deepest hunger? It may interest you to find out that I am 3,000 miles away from the Carolinas and was visiting a new Bible study in Los Angeles when they played that sermon on CD. It just so happens to have been recorded by a guest speaker at Chris's church in the Carolinas. Yes, a message by a pastor speaking at Chris's church helped me gain understanding and find healing so I can give Chris a chance. Now, that is so like my life.

Coincidence?

Only time will tell us.

The next time I continue in this book will hopefully be its conclusion, sharing the love story God was actually writing on my behalf. I have to just be along for the ride, recording its events, rather than trying to dictate anymore what God is up to. Thank you for sharing this journey with me.

CHAPTER SIXTEEN
My Finally!

Cheryl's Journal (1994)

> God: "Your desire is a natural desire. Yet, like
> everything else, it must fall into place by My timing, not
> yours."

Praise God I had no idea in 1994 it would take this long. As I begin this chapter, it's 2011.

A few months before my trip to visit my family and Chris, a woman at a prayer group sensed I should leave all guys who've hurt me behind because God was ushering in someone new. The thought of Chris flitted across my mind as being that "someone new," but I'd been so burned at this point by the words people prophesied. I thought, *God, am I supposed to believe this one? Is this the first recent, accurate word about this situation while the rest are erroneous?* I was still not ready to give up Dylan at the time. So, I wrote it down and put it away in my journal.

Sometime before this, I told a friend I could see the end of this story coming a mile away. I would not end up with Dylan. I would end up with Chris but that it wasn't what I naturally wanted. I knew saying those words made no sense in the face of all the "confirmations" regarding Dylan, but I had a feeling God had a completely different story in mind than the one I thought He was writing.

Before my trip to spend time with Chris in person, I wrote a prayer:

Cheryl's Journal (November 2010)
It's still a mystery to me what You want from me with Chris, if it's the right move or not. I can only walk through the door. I do so, blindly, and just simply holding Your hand. That's probably what You've wanted all along, huh? I'd much rather join Your story than ask You to bless mine. You're a much better writer. In Never the Bride, *God asks Jessie to give up some of her dreams so that God's dreams can take their place. That's what I want to do. Who knew I could learn from my own story, my own character's journey after I wrote it?*

A Time of Thanksgiving

The journey with Chris began when I finally made my way to the Carolinas to reacquaint with him during my Thanksgiving trip to see my family. At the airport before flying out, I wrote in my journal: "Is this the beginning of a life-changing trip? There's a quietness in my spirit that says this is where I am headed."

The first trip was two weeks. Before I left for the trip, I went to a prayer meeting that had two prophetic words for me that seemed to be about this situation. First, one lady got a picture that indicated God was trying to move me forward swiftly, but that I stopped the forward motion to try to make myself more comfortable. God was calling me to "just go" and to stop trying to control everything. That sounded familiar to me.

Another woman saw a picture of a clock that showed ten till nine.

She said, "It's almost time." She felt it meant God was about to change my life and that the time was almost here, but she felt puzzled about why the time on the clock was ten till nine. I knew that Chris and I had our first date planned to begin at nine a.m. I wondered if this meant God was leading me into this with him.

I'll admit: it was a rough beginning. Chris and I spent lots of time together for two weeks. Our first real date was sixteen hours long. I wasn't the most cooperative participant, and my heart was still in pain from Dylan. God bless Chris for understanding that! Every step of the way, he had such great compassion for where I was at and didn't try to push me.

I went to a service with him where he was playing praise music. A woman in the crowd came up and prayed for me. She sensed a picture from God in her spirit: she saw a large block of ice that was frozen but would melt into a puddle of water. She felt whatever had been hard was going to melt and that God was going to break whatever needed to be broken. Given that I felt like an "ice cube" with Chris, I knew it was symbolic of me. I needed God to help *and* heal me so I could warm up to this situation and this man.

The love, care, and patience that Chris showed me, despite my behavior, encouraged me to press through, even though at first I had a hard time believing this was the right road. I could see he was a genuine, wonderful, caring man, completely sold out to God. He also understood, despite his foreign missionary heart, that I had the same heart except specifically for Hollywood, California, with no plans to move to Africa. My heart was to serve, maybe even try to change the world a little, through the entertainment industry. He knew I belonged here.

Chris told me he felt such confirmation when he went off on a retreat specifically to pray about whether to pursue me last April. He volunteered to relocate if things worked out with us, seeing the value in the ministry and calling on my life. He was a terrific listener, wanted to know who I was, what I had been through in life, and was open to sharing on a deep level, personally and spiritually. All of these traits were things I had been looking for, but my heart wasn't immediately cooperating. It wasn't "love at first sight." I wanted a clear, obvious answer right away. It didn't come. Then again, when has God ever done anything fast in my life?

I was encouraged that I enjoyed his family and felt comfortable with them. I could see our families had similar values and that his family enjoys spending time together as much as mine. The more time I spent with him, the easier it became to get to know him better. I also loved that we both have two sets of parents who are still together and clearly love each other. We come from a great legacy of committed marriages.

One of the most fun outings we had during my first two weeks was heading down to Charleston, South Carolina to scout potential locations for *Never the Bride*. It's a beautiful, romantic city. Since Chris is a photographer, it was fun to welcome him into my moviemaking life on a story I sensed could turn out to be about us.

Despite my early reservations, still, in the back of my mind, something told me not to give up too soon. I left that two-week trip knowing he was a cool guy, but not yet sure he was right for me. I wanted to take the two weeks between trips, before I'd be back in the Carolinas for Christmas, to pray and seek God about what He had in mind for us.

Truthfully, the problem was that I still needed a miracle heart healing.

The Healing

Two days before heading back to Charlotte for the next three-week trip, I went on a prayer retreat alone. Taking about five hours to myself, I prayed about Chris and me, and what God's will was for our lives. I didn't get anything specific, but an unexplainable peace showed up—a peace I hadn't felt so far. In fact, it was during that prayer time I began to look forward to seeing him again.

I knew there were still some residual issues in my heart with Dylan. I went to another event where Chris was playing music. A man walked up to me in the church lobby and said, "God has been pressing me to come tell you something. He has a big healing in store for you. It's something you may feel is impossible, but God can do it." My foot had still been hurting since the surgery, and it was especially bothering me that night. When I went back to my seat, I told God if I had to choose, I would much rather He bless me with an emotional healing over the past year than a physical healing. That's saying a lot; I'm still in pain with most steps I take a year and a half after surgery.

The next day I had the chance to see friends who are like my second family and update them about what had been going on the past year of my life. It was a watershed day. At first, it scared me how much everything still hurt. I thought, "What business do I have trying to give Chris a chance when I'm still clearly such a mess over Dylan?" Then, something amazing happened. In sharing my story with them, I started to see so clearly how well Chris had treated me this whole time—how Christ-like. If I were to guess who God may be writing into my story, it would be Chris. Not because there's anything wrong with Dylan but because Chris was made so right for me and was God's chosen.

The Loud Confirmation

The next morning, I knew I had turned a corner and felt remarkably better. Since then, now months later, I haven't cried over Dylan again. The volume of emotion may have scared me at the time, but it was a cleansing time of healing when God was doing a mighty work. It was the same work He promised to me, prophetically, the night before. That was probably the fastest time between a prophecy and its answer in reality I've ever experienced.

That morning, I met Chris at his church. I was so excited to see him and felt completely different in all the best ways. I started to feel hope this would work. After the service, I went to the church's prophetic prayer ministry. That morning, they were only taking visitors. So, Chris went off to the bookstore to get me a book while I privately went to the prayer session. It's set up where you sit at a table with a few strangers. You don't give them your prayer requests. Instead, they just start praying and speaking over you anything they feel led by the Holy Spirit to pray. As you've read many times in this book, I've had interesting prophetic encounters. Because of the erroneous words over the past year, I went into this with caution and low expectations. That's when God surprised me. It was one of the most specific prayer times I've ever heard. It cut straight through to the heart of what I had been wrestling with in my life. To follow is what they prayed over me, mixed with the thoughts I had during the prayer:

One woman said, "God sees the decision-making time you are in. You haven't had the firm answer in your heart just yet, but God will reveal this answer through His Holy Spirit. He's revealing these things you have been asking Him for. The answer came in a way you didn't readily recognize. Keep your faith and hope strong because God is opening up the answer to you about what you've been asking for."

Privately, I thought about how I've been praying about this decision regarding Chris. Should we advance to a real relationship? Is he the right person for me? I'd been praying for a husband for a long time. Where at first, I had been rejecting the idea, I wondered if they were confirming God, indeed, was pointing him out and yet, so far, I hadn't recognized it.

Then next person praying said, "You've been seeking, and he who seeks finds. You've been seeking relationship, but the problem is you've been running around with a magnifying glass, looking at the situation too closely for all its little details. God wants you to back up and just look at the big picture. If you don't, you could miss it. Back up so He can show you His perspective. You can overlook what He has for you if you're too close."

At this point, I quietly pondered how I had been trying to figure out all the details. How will this work with Chris? We live on opposite sides of the country. What would he do in Los Angeles if he follows me here? I had concerns I wanted answers to before I'd even given the relationship a chance to start. I knew God's illustration of the magnifying glass was absolutely true. So far in this prayer session, I had confirmation in my spirit that they were hearing from God accurately for me.

They continued, "You have been looking for something actively. This thing that you've been seeking is right in front of your face. It's been there all this time, but now it's revealed."

I've been looking for my husband. Chris is right in front of my face, here and now, ready for a relationship with me. I've known him a long time, as we met fourteen years ago. By this point, I'm feeling super sure they are prophetically praying about Chris.

Then one guy pipes up and says, "I'm going out on a limb here and going to be so bold to say that what you've been seeking is your lifelong companion. You know him. He's already here. You have questions. Let God give you the impression of this most meaningful and complete relationship so He can move you into a very meaningful future."

Wow. I sat stunned for a few moments then thanked them for their prayers.

When I left the prayer session, I privately thanked God for being so clear and so specific. This prayer session left little room for error in its interpretation. I so appreciated that, considering all the times I'd been burned by prophecies that were too vague to discern accurately or that were wrong or off. I'd rather have mistakes come through at times than not ever hear from God this way at all. I was so grateful God was clear, confirming, and giving me my marching orders straight into Chris's heart.

I so appreciated the specific acknowledgment that this man was already in my life, and that I was the one with questions. By this point, Chris was not the one questioning us. I was. I found out later there were reasons he was so sure about us before I even stepped foot back into the Carolinas. He will have the chance to share his side of our story with you as well. It gave me great comfort to know I could walk through this door and not mess up God's plan for my life. I'd be walking straight into His plan.

When I joined Chris at the bookstore—where he lovingly waited in the longest line ever to get me a free visitor book—he asked how the prayer session went. I just smiled and said, "Awesome. Someday, I will tell you about it." I held this giant secret in my heart about what God just confirmed to me about us. I knew I could walk boldly into a relationship with him.

Additional *Never the Bride* Parallels

As I pondered Jessie's story in *Never the Bride,* and who I wrote her husband to be, I saw more parallels. He had to first get to know Jessie by computer and her blog. When Chris was first getting to know me again, it was over Facebook and other things available about me on the Internet. We weren't talking on the phone yet so it was all electronic communication. Jessie's future husband writes to her, and gets to know her at this same distance, falling for her even without spending time with her in person. He also kept writing about how much he understood her feelings of loneliness from her blogs. Chris did the same with me, regarding emails I wrote to answer his questions about past relationships.

They also have a history from the past, like Chris and I did. They are around the same age. Their names start with the same letter, which I made that choice deliberately when naming Jessie's man. Chris is savvy with computers. He's even his sister's computer fix-it guy. That's what Jessie's future guy does for a living.

Jessie's guy was so sure of her—before they'd even had their first date—that he renovated a house the way she'd like once they got married. In Chris's case, he was already researching Los Angeles for a potential move and got a new car in preparation for that move before we'd even been on our first date. Now, that's assurance!

Meanwhile, Chris felt like he had signposts that encouraged him to wait for me. In *Never the Bride*, Jessie's real guy is the one getting signposts (a.k.a. God Winks).

Additionally, Jessie had the hardest time giving up her "best friend." As we know, so did I. God told her He had someone else for her. The night Jessie has to face this loss is the same night God reveals who Jessie is supposed to be with. There's no wait time for her. I felt the same way as I was giving up Dylan to make room for Chris. I had no gap between. This was the only time in my life where God gave me hope in someone new as I experienced the loss of someone else. Though I can't say I felt ready for it, and I felt bad for putting my character through such a whiplash turnaround. In reality, this was extremely hard. I joked with God about how I wrote quite a challenge for Jessie without realizing it!

Ironically, my co-author, Rene Gutteridge, on the novel version of *Never the Bride* had described Jessie's engagement ring as having three diamonds on it. Little did she know the engagement ring I would inherit from my grandmother over a year later—after she penned that detail—would have three diamonds in it.

I had penned *Finally the One*, the sequel to *Never the Bride*, shortly before Chris and I reconnected. Many things from that story paralleled Chris and I as well, and I hadn't been in touch with him yet. I have no doubt God was setting me up and wanted me to have these works written in advance so I could then watch His writing hand unfold in such astounding ways.

The biggest parallel of course is that Chris waited so patiently for me, even in the face of multiple rejections. He respected every single boundary I put up. He stood firm and waited for me to be ready for him. I'm so grateful he didn't give up on me. As Chris will tell you, this is unusual for him. Historically, he never would have stuck it out with a girl who gave him so little encouragement in his pursuit. Chris knows the Lord quite well, hears His voice, and knew what he was supposed to do regardless of my behavior. He trusted God to work it out from day one.

The Obvious Pursuit

The difference in how Chris behaved from the five best guy friends I had over the past seven years is striking! His pursuit was clear, obvious, and I never had to question what he was thinking or feeling about us. He told me with his own mouth. I've never experienced anything like this in my life.

I am grateful to be beyond the repeat of friendships that landed in heartache. If you happen to be a guy reading this: please be protective of the hearts of your female friends and make sure you're clear with your intentions.

Most likely, ladies, if you are the one forced to bring up the question if a friendship is going anywhere, the guy is not pursuing you. It's still good to ask so you don't spend too much time in a friendship that is just that: a platonic friendship. Unless that's all you want and not marriage, but if you're reading this book, I doubt you're in that category.

I echo the advice of my friend who went through the same thing. She was right: it feels very different to be with someone who has the capacity to love you. There is no comparison. Save your heart the additional pain and keep your friendships with guys from becoming emotional attachments, if there is no pursuit for your heart.

The Prophetic Set-Up

I noticed one important thing that was different about how prophecy was used in this version of my story as opposed to other times, like with Dylan, when I thought God was speaking. This time, most of the prophetic words seemed to confirm what was already happening in my life. They showed me I was on the right track, rather than being like "fortune-telling" of what's to come. If anything was revealing the future, I didn't know it for sure until after it happened. This is an important distinction and ties to the Bible's word about how we prophesy in part. (See 1 Corinthians 13:9.) Too often we take prophecy as a whole and assume it's the complete picture, yet it almost never is.

We also may feel tempted to fill in the blanks ourselves before God shows us what a prophecy actually means.

In this case, God kept leading me down the path I was already on by showing me payoffs to past prophecies, like little signposts along the way. Any new prophetic words were confirming things that were already taking place.

I loved every moment a signpost showed up. I have a few more examples for you. While some of these words or pictures were given to me up to eight years ago, I had no way to know what they meant until God showed me when they came to pass.

Remember the pool party dream from the "Foreshadowing" chapter? Let's look at some of the symbolism first then the payoffs. I knew that dream was about my future husband. In the dream, the man was someone I knew from the past. It showed that once I was with him, my interest in him would take me by surprise because it wasn't an interest that was initially there. It showed this was a guy who would be able to hear God's voice concerning me and would obey. There was also an interesting symbol about how I was being restored, including Christmas and photo losses.

Here are some of the payoffs: Chris was someone I knew in the past and didn't date. True to the story of that dream, my interest while getting reacquainted with him took me by surprise. Chris's birthday is on Christmas Day, and we took a bunch of photos over Christmas, including putting ourselves in front of the Christmas tree because we both continuously felt like we were each other's Christmas gifts. Because we'd both spent so many painful Christmas seasons alone, this particular Christmas felt like a time of restoration for both of us.

Remember my 2003 journal entry where God asked about my husband, "Do you want a gift before it's wrapped?" How suitable God chose Christmas to solidify our relationship. We had already been charting our love story through 2,000 photos between Thanksgiving and Christmas. It seemed like redemption for all the time that had passed during our quest for love.

One of the first dreams about my future husband showed that a guy would come to me on Easter. He would show up and I was to wait in anticipation for him. Ironically, Easter 2010 was when our email friendship initially kicked up. Days after we first reconnected over Facebook, I flew to Florida for Easter to see my family. Chris started sending me long, thoughtful notes and being clear that he wanted to get to know me, including where I was with romantic relationships. I even told my sister at the time that I sensed he was interested in me. So our initial beginning, indeed, was during Easter. For a while after that dream in 2004, I was watchful around Easter, hoping something would happen. After a few years, I gave up. As it turns out, it was indeed our true beginning, even if it took a while for me to figure that out. Again, it was a neat signpost to look back on later and realize how much God intricately wove this story together and foreshadowed it for me in ways I couldn't completely understand until God wanted me to see it all.

Another cool signpost ties to how I wrote the first chapter of this book. It came from the following excerpt:

> *I am not suggesting you sign up for this Boot Camp because I think you need a lot more preparation before you're worthy of love and marriage. However, if you're like me, you have nothing better to do while waiting for that "in the flesh" husband to arrive. At your doorstep. Sporting a bow. (Like a Christmas bow because anything else would be creepy.)*

When I was home for Christmas, Chris drove down to Florida to join us for some family time at my sister's house. Imagine my surprise when he drives up, gets out of the car and steps out wearing a Christmas bow. I have no doubt the Holy Spirit led him to do such an adorable thing that he didn't know was a God Wink to me.

In the first chapter, I also wrote:

What's to say that by the time I finish this book, its title, Finally the Bride, *won't have a dual meaning? Not just finally the bride of Christ, but also, finally a real flesh-and-blood bride in a real white dress because at this point I still qualify to wear one. (Yes, I am well on my way to becoming the 40-year-old virgin. That is not a title I'm hoping to win. "Did you hear that, God? I have deadlines. So far, you've blown them all. Please, don't blow this one!")*

I have to thank God for listening to this deadline I requested so comically, as I will get married while I'm still 39. (Nothing like waiting for the last minute, God! Thank You, nonetheless.)

In 2003 when God gave the woman at a prayer meeting words about how I would one day get married, she included that, "Once it starts, it will go quickly." Keeping this in mind helped me not completely freak out over the pace of our courtship. Also, in 2004, I wrote down my sense that my future husband already knew my name. I questioned, *Is this a stranger who was given the name of his future wife, or does it mean I already know this person and neither of us realize we're going to marry each other?* Only time would tell.

You know how I've mentioned occasionally God has used signs as fun little God Winks? On my second trip home, Chris and I were on our way to lunch. We drove by a sign that said, "IMURBOAZ" meaning "I'm your Boaz." I smiled and laughed internally so as not to call attention to anything. Inside, I asked God, "Are you telling me Chris is my Boaz, like Boaz was to Ruth? My earthly protector and provider?" I wanted to take a picture, but it would have been too hard to explain to Chris, and we still weren't in an official relationship yet.

After New Years, we were sightseeing and happened upon a store called Ruby's Gift. I made him pose under the sign so I could take his picture, since I considered him to be my gift, and Ruby was one of God's nicknames for me.

The day that we shared our first kiss was a fun day trip to the mountains to go to the Biltmore Estate. While there, we popped into a Christmas store where I saw a rack of Christmas ornaments with people's names on them. Suddenly, I heard in my spirit, "Check out the names. Your name and Chris's name are beside each other." Wondering if I heard right, I swung the rack around and sure enough, one said, "Cheryl" and the one beside it said "Chris." Naturally, we photographed this.

The last story I'd like to share for this section is about how in 2004, one of my closest friends, Susan Rohrer, had what's proven to be a prophetic dream about my future husband. She said he was a cute guy with brown hair, was about 5' 10", and that when I walked in the room, he watched me with such love and simply said, "Wow." Since that day she's been waiting for there to be that guy in my life who would consider me a "Wow." She hadn't seen that look or feeling from any of those guys I liked since that dream. Over Christmas, Chris constantly said "Wow" when he'd look at me. He made his interest and attraction to me known. I loved that he didn't hide it and had no embarrassment over showing me he felt I was a "Wow." Susan loved hearing this story and felt like it belonged on the long list of confirmations lining up this story.

True Love

Until this point in my life, to my knowledge, no guy has ever been in love with me. I'm not aware of anyone who felt that strongly about me, whether I dated them or not. None of my boyfriends ever said, "I love you." One guy wrote it in a note, but I figured out quickly he didn't mean it when he broke up with me a few weeks later—right before Valentines Day.

Once Chris and I turned a new corner and knew for sure we wanted to be in a relationship, I knew inside I wasn't ready to say "this is love." I was a little concerned about how I'd respond if he said it to me and I wasn't ready to say it in return. Then on January 1, 2011, I was saying good-bye to him and saw something in his eyes that told me he loved me. I thought, *This is what it feels like when someone actually loves you.* Then I heard in my spirit, "he's going to tell you." Just then, he took my face in his hands and said, "Cheryl McKay, I love you." So, what was my response?

I started crying.

Unexpected reaction, no doubt. I told him no one had ever said that to me before. I said I appreciated how every step of the way with us, he'd been a great leader. I think I needed the assurance of his love to finally let down all the walls around my heart. I had to be protected so much of my life. He was letting me know it was safe. Just a few days later, I knew I loved him. It was the first time in my life that love was ever mutual. It was the most awesome feeling. I think back to an earlier chapter when I wrote: "If I were able to walk into a relationship that I had no doubt God had set up, I believe true love would follow." I had no idea how right I'd turn out to be. I'm grateful God, indeed, worked with me this way.

Heading Toward Marriage

Before my trip, in a prayer meeting, a friend told me to be on the lookout for a pond or an area we'd go to that had water. I happened along this entry in my journal a couple days before the end of this trip and thought, *Hmm. That hasn't happened yet, and it's almost time to head home.* Chris asked if we could take my last day in town to pray about us, our timing, and the future. He wanted to take me to this place where he used to always pray for his future wife.

When we arrived at this location, we walked over the crest of a hill, and there was a beautiful pond or lake. I knew in that moment this was the place the lady referenced. Again, God gave me another comforting signpost of being on the right track. We spent three hours on the docks by the water—with Chris playing praise songs on his guitar—singing and praying together. It was the first time he referred to me as his wife, and we knew one day we would get married.

The Engagement

Chris had never been to California before, so we decided he should come out in time for Valentines Day. We'd both had our share of painful Valentines Days and looked forward to celebrating with each other.

While I knew the proposal was coming because we'd already talked about wedding plans, I wasn't sure what he was up to. He planned it for Friday, February 18, 2011, which was technically our three-month anniversary, even though we'd been talking for six months before our first date. He asked if he could plan the day for himself for our anniversary without me knowing how we'd celebrate.

As we left my apartment, he plugged an address into my GPS. We pull into a neighborhood, park the car, and walk up to an apartment door where he calls someone. I'm thinking, *Who on earth does he know in Los Angeles and what are we doing here?* A lady comes up, all excited to see us, and notices the confused look on my face. I have no idea who she is or why we're coming to see her for our anniversary. Turns out, this is the photographer he shoots weddings with in Charlotte. She just so happened to be in Los Angeles. We were picking her up to take her with us to do "couple's photos" (a.k.a. engagement and "capture the proposal" photos, though I don't know this yet.)

He then guides me to take us to the Santa Monica pier, which for eleven years now has been my favorite place in Los Angeles. I have spent many-a-day praying for my "future husband," not knowing who he'd be, at this beach. We had a blast for a couple of hours being silly, romantic, and creative, posing for photos.

Eventually, we landed at the end of the pier that overlooks the Pacific, Catalina Island, Malibu, and the mountains. He gets down on one knee, pulls out a ring box, opens it. Inside, it holds a beautiful wedding band that so perfectly matches my grandmother's precious engagement ring. (I'm sad she won't be there in person to share my wedding day, but I praise God for this special way for her to participate.) Chris did a great job finding a beautiful complement to her ring when he chose my wedding band. Inside the ring box held several personalized M&Ms with the request, "Will You Marry Me?" The M&Ms also shouted, "I want you!!!" and "I choose you!!!" Chris is well aware I've spent years feeling not chosen or wanted. Remember: the inspiration for my script and novel, *Never the Bride*, started off by my complaint that I've never been anybody's choice. Yes, that self-pity moment that made me laugh at myself and ask God, "This is going in a script, isn't it?" Chris wanted to make sure I know that I am the only choice for him.

Adorably, the man who proposes to my character Jessie in *Never the Bride* uses personalized M&Ms to propose. It was so fun to be living out my "fictional" dream yet, it was real and true, and the man behind the question truly loves me, wants me, and chooses me. Our awesome photographer captured this magical moment on this beautiful pier as I cried, receiving this ring. Naturally, I said yes about ninety times.

I loved hearing how Chris plotted with my sister, my parents, and one of my best friends as he was putting this all together.

There were days in my journey I'd struggled to keep hope alive that I would find someone to love and cherish for the rest of my life. No doubt I had to wait a long time for his arrival, but I can honestly say, Chris was well worth the wait.

I recall writing in an earlier chapter, long before Chris's arrival, the following encouragement for us all:

> *"Once you find out what God is writing for the romantic-comedy script of your life, you will be able to look back and trace clues, winks, nods, and hints... You may not realize what part you're playing as you're playing it. God may shield your eyes from seeing everything clearly until the right time. Trust that He is at work, even when His foreshadowing fingers are not making themselves known."*

I had no idea how true that statement would become to my own story.

I'm grateful God worked this way, and that now I can see it!

Did you notice my father's insight through prayer was right? I wasn't alone anymore by Valentines Day 2011!

The Wedding

Within a couple days of our engagement, we had a date set: May 14, 2011.

Remember my story about going on a retreat to be alone with God after I took a break from Dylan? That retreat was from May 12-14, 2010. I had absolutely no idea, when I left that retreat center praying about my future mate—or more accurately my "missing mate"—exactly one year later would be my wedding date.

When I wrote the script version of *Never the Bride*, I wrote that Jessie gets married at her in-laws' place. I couldn't have predicted that I'd marry someone whose family has a house big enough and nice enough to hold a wedding. Chris's whole family had a hand in building his sister's ranch home, based on her vision and designs. The location was so perfect and stunningly beautiful! Chris never realized all those hours he spent putting floorboard down that he was building the floor his future bride would walk on toward him.

Our wedding day was picture-perfect. The ceremony was both touching and fun, and Chris's humor at the altar went a long way toward keeping me calm. The day showed me how much better of a romance writer God is than I am. I was filled with a sense of gratefulness for all the times God overrode my desires in favor of His own. I know He could do that because I surrendered the pen of my love story to Him. I could have said "no" to His desires for my life. I'm grateful He kept me on His path, playing a role in the story He was writing. I could have missed out!

We had our ceremony on a ranch where there are ten horses. The ceremony was in a beautiful living room with a stone fireplace that had a cross built into it. I got to walk down that aisle toward the most amazing man God could have ever given to me. We spoke personal words to each other before the formal vows. We had our reception in the sunroom and on the deck that overlooks the horse corrals. During the reception, we had a chance to share slices of our love story with everyone through a video we shot a few days before the wedding.

It felt like living a fairy tale, the fictional life I'd written for Jessie. Except this time, I got to walk through it in my own life, not just write about it on paper, vicariously living through a character. We could feel the power of answered prayers all day. Many who joined us that day had been our prayer warriors before we knew what God was up to with us.

One of the biggest answered prayers for me was having my dad there. In September 2004, when my dad needed to have open-heart surgery, I posted a list of goals and dreams on his bedpost at the hospital. Number one on that list was "walk Cheryl down the aisle." I wanted to give him many reasons to stick around and survive the surgery. A nurse asked me, "So, when are you getting married?" I said, "I have no idea, but my precious dad better be here for it!" So dancing with my dad at my wedding was a beautiful dream come true for me. It was also awesome to share the day with my mom and all of her siblings. The last time I'd seen them was during my grandmother's final day of life, then her funeral when I inherited her engagement ring.

My dear husband surprised me by writing me a song: "I Love My Baby." Its world premiere was at our wedding reception with his live band.

We left our reception that day knowing we were loved and supported by some of the best family and friends around.

The List

Remember the list I made in the chapter titled Just How Good of a Writer is God (Doesn't He Need my Suggestions)? It was astounding for me to go back to the lists of what I desired in a mate and find that Chris matches with spot-on accuracy.

Even the concerns I had over what I'd have to give up once

married have been moot—the list I wrote about "why it's great to be single." God tailored my man so specifically that even what I thought would bother me hasn't been a problem. My man doesn't snore. After the first month of getting used to each other, I was able to sleep well next to him, sometimes even falling asleep faster than he does. I enjoy spending money on lingerie and surprising him, or calling home to check in. He's fantastic at giving me my space to write. He doesn't throw off my apartment organization, and he always lowers the toilet seat. A bonus is my husband likes to watch eighties sitcoms, so I still get to watch them, to lull me to sleep at night. He relocated to Los Angeles for me, so I could keep working as a screenwriter.

God knew what He was doing when He chose Chris for me. Long before I knew it would turn out to be Chris, I wrote in this book that I would love to have a man who could write romantic songs for me. Chris has and continues to do so. I was amazed to see how much God has given me the desires of my heart.

I want to take a moment to honor this man and share a slice of who he is with you. Chris is patient, kind, servant-hearted, a great listener, sold out to God, one who hears the Holy Spirit's leading and believes God still speaks today. He's loving, supportive, protective, romantic, thoughtful, and sensitive. He knows how to laugh and has a good sense of humor. He's caring, empathetic, doesn't like to see me in pain, is a prayer warrior, and has a strong faith. He's a family man. He is my spiritual leader and ends every day praying over me. He's a good sport. No matter how silly my ideas may be, he enjoys just joining me for the adventure. He shares many of my same hobbies, like being outside, exploring, and taking photos to capture life's important and memorable moments.

I don't ever feel like I have to entertain him or be fun enough for him to like me. He already does. I don't feel any pressure around him like I did around other guys I wanted to win over. He already enjoys me, already wants me, and I can just relax and be myself. He has the most beautiful heart I've ever known and I am truly blessed to be his wife. He is so much more than I ever could have asked for or imagined that I'd receive. Chris shows me why God knows best. I can't thank God enough for what He's done in bringing us together. Chris is my gift from God in so many ways. I adore him and this new family I've married into.

Trust God at All Costs

I know this journey you are on is hard. I've walked it, all thirty-nine years of it. If you choose to surrender your pen to God, you will probably face the odd looks and stares from your friends or family members who won't understand your choices. They may think you're not doing enough to "make this happen" on your own. I tried it both ways. I couldn't make something happen, no matter how hard I tried. It wasn't until I surrendered that area of my life to God that God chose to move. I'm sorry if the speed with which God worked in my life isn't overly encouraging, but at least it proves God has been faithful to His promises to me, regardless of how long it took Him. Maybe I should say regardless of how long it took me to surrender to His will for me.

I definitely had to withstand my share of ridicule. It wasn't just from some well-meaning people I knew who just wanted my life to move forward faster than it was, but also from strangers who read articles I wrote about singleness. One person made fun of me, quipping about how long it must have been since I'd been on a date. This person disagreed with my opinion about waiting on God for His help in this area of life. I may come across to some as crazy as Noah building an ark in a time when no one had even heard of rain yet, but I had to obey how I felt God was leading me.

Yes, I failed along the way and made some mistakes, but overall, I knew the only love story worth living was the one God was writing. Now that I know the story He's penning, I'm so glad I trusted in that. What good would it have done me, like the article reader expressed, if I had dated a bunch of guys on the west coast when God knew all along my future husband was on the east coast? I'm glad that for those seven and a half years, I didn't date other people or hop online to try to find someone.

It couldn't have happened any sooner than it did. Remember that "baking pie" word? God was working independent of me in Chris's life, too, preparing him for me. Well, to be honest, I suppose it could have happened about six months sooner if I had been open to it when Chris first asked me to consider a relationship. Again, had I cooperated, that pastor's prophetic time line could very well have been true—I could have been married by October. Ironically, our wedding was just shy of six months after our first date, which could have put our wedding close to October 25, 2010.

I don't regret the time lost. I know God did a good and mighty, healing work in me and has been building my testimony along the way, even in the mistakes I made that so strikingly parallel those I wrote my character Jessie making. I guess one bonus is that it makes for a better story, doesn't it? (Yeah, thanks for allowing all the drama, God!) Thankfully, Chris didn't jump ship from our story out of discouragement because of my slowness to hop on board with him.

The Commission
Chris and I both have a heart to be in ministry together and speak to other people about God and our story. In 2007, God gave me a commission about my future marriage:

> *Cheryl's Journal (August 2007)*
> *"You will be a praying couple. You will be a ministry couple. My Spirit will flow actively through you both. You both are leaders for My Kingdom, My sheep, those who need to hear but don't."*

I'm excited about our future.

I'm excited that Chris, as a missionary, is so suited for this work ahead of us. It will be an adventure.

Chris and I are on a special journey together, and we have a sense that God will use our story and the two of us to help others.

I have the feeling this is only the beginning.

CHAPTER SEVENTEEN

His Finally!
by Christopher Price

WANTED: WIFE

Single, godly, late 30s male seeks amazing,
beautiful, godly wife.
I've been waiting on God's best: someone who I can love and be
attracted to spiritually, emotionally, and physically. Someone that
I can serve Him together with and enjoy spending the rest of my
life with. If this is you, please HURRY UP AND MAKE
YOURSELF KNOWN!!! I'M TIRED OF WAITING!!!

So, have you ever felt like posting an ad like this? If you're single and you have a desire to be married, I imagine the thought has crossed your mind a time or twenty like it had mine. Are you tired of waiting for "the one" to show up in your life, but you don't want to just find anyone? You know, one who's nice, who you think you can get along with, and marry just for the sake of being married?

Do you feel like God has someone handpicked for you, but you're just tired of waiting an eternity for Him to bring him or her along? Read on then, because there is hope yet! I, too, was in this singles' boat wanting so badly to get out of it. I was caught in this same situation: wanting the right one for me, but not being willing to settle for less than God's best.

My name is Chris Price, and as of writing this chapter, I'm still considered a newlywed with Cheryl. I wanted to share a little of my side of our journey with you to give you hope. I think guys wanting to be married will relate to what I have to share. However, ladies, don't check out on me at this point as I have some specific things to share with you concerning finding the "right" guy. So hang in there with me and we'll go on this journey together.

Singlehood

Single. What does that mean to you? Do you feel like you have a gigantic "S" tattooed on your forehead that lets everyone know you don't have someone special in your life? Maybe you have heard the same advice from well-meaning friends like I did. Friends give pearls of wisdom such as, "You're just too picky," or "You need to lower your standards a little, then you'll find someone." Or maybe you've heard some sage gems like, "You need to buy some new clothes and dress more hip. Try to look younger." Or maybe you've heard my personal favorite, "You have commitment issues."

I started thinking: *Maybe I do have commitment issues because I've been out with several girls and none of them felt right to me as my potential wife.* I even started wondering what was wrong with me. Everyone else seemed able to find someone (and they were almost half my age). *Why can't I find someone?*

In hindsight, nothing was wrong with me. I didn't have commitment issues, and I didn't need to lower my standards. I wasn't waiting on the next *America's Top Model* to come along. I simply wanted the *right* person for me, someone that I was attracted to spiritually, emotionally, *and* physically. Was that too much to ask? Evidently, it wasn't, because that's *exactly* what God gave me.

Let's look at a few more things that you may relate to about being single.

If you're in your thirties or early forties and still single, did you ever get tired of going to church and not fitting in anywhere? You were too old for the college and careers class, but you felt a little out of place in the forty-five and above singles class. No offense to them! It was a great class and I knew some great people there, but I just felt like I didn't really fit anywhere.

How about dating? I have never been big on dating just for the sake of dating. I always looked at dating as a way to narrow the field to find my wife. It seemed like I was always on the lookout for her. You know what I mean. Every time you go to a group event you wonder, "Will *she* be here tonight?" It was a never-ending feeling, walking into a new place or new group of people and keeping my eyes peeled for the "one" who caught my eye—or checking to see if I caught *her* eye. I even went through a dry spell of feeling like I was the invisible man where no girl ever noticed me, not even the ones I wouldn't consider going out with.

If I did catch someone's eye, it was short-lived because of the girl repellent I was wearing. Yeah, you heard me. Girl repellent. It was as if any girl who initially seemed interested was mysteriously—and suddenly—uninterested. I showered regularly, dressed well, and even gave myself the self-administered breath test. Still, they seemed to make themselves scarce. I just couldn't figure out why no girl was interested in me. Now, I realize that God was simply keeping me from any distractions and was saving me for Cheryl. He was answering a prayer of mine to not get derailed from finding my wife. So God was helping me, but in my frustration I didn't see it that way.

Small Faith-Builders

Thankfully, God did give me some faith-builders along the way. One came after a particularly hard breakup. I was in my early twenties and asked God, point-blank, if He had someone for me or if it was just going to be Him and me. After I prayed this, He flooded me with this incredible peace and I instantly went from crying to laughing. This immediate rush of peace was God's way of telling me that He did have someone for me. I carried this promise with me for years, before the fulfillment manifested in my life. It gave me hope and strength to wait for His best.

A few years later, when my faith was beginning to wane a bit, I asked God a question as I was taking a stroll down the beach. Looking up, I prayed to ask if He had a particular wife in mind for me. As soon as my eyes fell back to the sand, in front of me I saw two unique footprints that triggered an instant spiritual download. I had a revelation that my wife was going to be someone who was equal to me — in calling and desire to reach people for Christ — and that we would seem to be going in two different directions. However, we would meet in a God-ordained encounter. Once we met, we would see that we were actually going in the same direction in life on parallel paths and that the Lord just joined us.

One time, after more years of waiting, I was getting impatient and thought, *By golly, I'm gonna find me a wife!* Have you been there? So, I went where everyone else went to find a mate quickly. Yep, you guessed it: online.

I was two-thirds of the way through my Yahoo! personals ad when I felt the Lord speak to me. It was as if He tapped me on the shoulder and asked me, "What are you doing?" I answered, "Well, since You're taking forever, I'm going to find myself a wife. I'm tired of being single and apparently, You are not doing anything about it." Then He asked, "Don't you trust Me?" I sat and stewed for a moment before responding. "I do, but You are taking *forever* to bring her." He said, "Okay, go ahead and do it on your own, but you know how things have gone when you've taken charge and run ahead of Me. If you choose her this way, you will miss My best for you."

I sat for a few moments considering the situation and the decision before me. I *so* wanted God's best for me, but I was tired of doing life alone. However, I chose to continue to trust Him and His timing. As I was deleting my profile, I swear I heard Him chuckle.

Falling for Miss Wrong

Have you ever not paid attention to important signs or red flags about someone and gotten hurt? There were two times in my life when I wrote a list of what I was looking for in a wife. The first time, it included ten things, the tenth one being that she is a solid believer and follower of Jesus. Well, less than two months after making that list, I met a girl who was very attractive and interested in me. That was not a combination that I was used to at the time. She was incredible and she was *almost* everything that I was looking for. She was nine of the ten things I had written down. Can you guess which one of the ten she was not? She was *not* a solid believer and follower of Jesus. However, I was smitten and didn't heed that glaring red flag. That led to a fourteen-month rollercoaster ride that ended in disaster and a seriously broken heart for me.

Then there was the "friend" that I was interested in, but she just didn't see me *that way*. Actually, I was interested in a couple of girls who didn't see me as more than a friend. I even thought one of them was supposed to be my wife, but I was wrong, in similar ways Cheryl shared with you earlier.

Encouraging Signs Along the Way

One of the most amazing signs along my journey occurred the early morning of September 28, 2007. I had just stirred from sleep and started to slip back into R.E.M. when I saw a picture in my mind. I could see the scene of a tall, thin, dark-haired woman with long hair. She was dressed in a white wedding gown holding a bouquet of flowers, and she was looking down. She looked sad because she appeared to have been waiting a *really* long time for her groom to show up. However, the guy had just not arrived. I got the sense that she was almost ready to give up hope, but she was still holding on. Barely. I could see the hurt and the frustration on her face, without seeing the details of her face. So, she was unrecognizable to me.

I remember waking up from that dream asking, "God, what are you trying to tell me from that dream?" Then the realization hit me like a Mack truck—the vision I saw was my future wife. She was waiting on *me*. You see, before that dream, my prayers had been that the Lord would prepare my wife and bring her to me. I thought I was ready for marriage and that the hang-up was with *her*. I thought she was the one needing preparation. However, through the dream, God revealed that my future wife was the one who was ready, and that *I* was the one who needed to be prepared for her. From that time forward, I prayed that the Lord would prepare me for the wife He had for me.

After this dream, I launched a prayer campaign for my future bride. In addition to praying for my preparation, I also began to pray fervently that God would keep all the wrong guys away from her. I prayed that she would not give in to disappointment and just settle for someone who was not God's best for her—and the best was clearly *myself*. I did this every day for over a year because I felt compelled by God to pray for her. It was cool praying for my wife during this time because, even though I couldn't see her face to see who she was, I pictured the bride in my dream. This prayer campaign occurred from late 2007 through most of 2008.

Shortly after the dream of the bride, I was having coffee with a couple of friends. One said she had a dream about me. She saw me in my hometown of Charlotte, with a very pretty woman who was tall, thin and had long, dark hair. She said that she couldn't tell if the lady in her dream was my girlfriend or my wife. I thought to myself, "Well, I guess I can mark any blondes off my list of potential candidates." It was around this time that another friend of mine arranged for me to meet a friend of hers that she thought I would really like because we had similar interests. She had blonde hair.

I was thankful for the confirmation from God, that my wife would have dark hair, as I have always been more attracted to girls with long, dark-colored hair. So, her dream was a real encouragement to me and a confirmation of the dream about my bride.

Another little sign came one day when I was out for a jog and felt the Lord speak to me. I was on my last lap of the day when I had this soft little "knowing" in my heart. Just as I was nearing the finish line, I also felt like I was nearing the finish line of waiting and being prepared for my wife. It was an amazing sense of peace, serenity, and an inner knowing that things were about to change. I remember smiling in relief and praising God for what He was about to do in my life.

One of the last signs I had was that I was given two tickets to the Biltmore Estate. There were a few girls that I considered inviting to go with me on the trip. I also really had a sense in my spirit that whoever went with me would end up becoming my wife. However, after inviting a few girls to go with me and having no takers, I shelved the tickets until I felt prompted by God to invite someone again.

A Word of Caution

Shortly after these signs, I was introduced to a girl who seemed to have many of the same characteristics as the bride I saw in my dream. My gut instinct was that this was not "the one." However, we began hanging out as friends, which clouded my judgment. I became confused as to whether I should pursue this girl or not. After asking God for help and clarity in the situation, our relationship abruptly ended. The moral of the story is to go with your gut instinct because many times it's the Lord speaking to you. Also, just before the real answer comes, you will potentially run into a counterfeit.

A New Chapter

During this time of waiting, I continually prayed that the Lord would change me. However, I was not fully aware of the changes that still needed to take place. As I continued to pray earnestly for my wife and for my preparation, my life — its dreams, goals, desires, ministry, and relationships — began to unravel. Ministry opportunities were drying up. Others were getting to go on mission trips — not me. Musical opportunities, other than playing with a few worship bands, began to diminish. It was a frustrating time, where I felt like I didn't understand anything that was happening, but I knew that God was in it somehow.

So, the Lord began to take away almost every part of ministry that I enjoyed. He required me to lay down my dreams of being an evangelist and *musicianary*, a missionary who shares Jesus through music ministry. I'll admit this was a most painful process. It was literally like experiencing a death because it *was* the death of dreams I'd held onto and pursued for almost thirteen years. This was an intensely painful, three-month journey the Lord took me through.

Thankfully, toward the end of this process, I attended a conference at a church I was playing for, where the speaker did an entire talk about "turning the page" and "starting a new chapter" in life. He mentioned that many times, God — out of His mercy and love for us — will have to remove things, even sometimes rip things out of our hands, to place what He wants us to have in them.

Are you holding on too tightly to anything right now? Is there something that the Lord may be asking you to lay down so He can lead you into His best?

Thankfully, that sermon shed some understanding on what was going on, but it really didn't lessen the pain. I had no idea that this same preacher would play such a vital role in helping Cheryl heal and consider me.

I have learned through experience that, many times, God will bring us to the point of laying down our preconceived notions or expectations of what our lives should be like before He brings what we should have. I had a preconceived image in my head of what my life should look like, what I would be doing for ministry, and what type of woman I would marry. Many times God has to bring us to a place of laying it all down—and I mean *all* down, where He dismantles our lives. Then He can put us back together the way He wants us to be.

We can have our dreams that we believe are straight from God, and plan and strive to reach them all we want. In the end, God is the one who will bring it to pass or not. Proverbs 16:9 says, "In their hearts humans plan their course, but the LORD establishes their steps." Proverbs 19:21 says, "Many are the plans in a person's heart, but it is the LORD's purpose that prevails."

I believe that the Lord's purpose for our lives is awesome. I am equally amazed that He will bring people into our lives and do great things in us if we will get out of His way. Pay attention to what He is doing.

A Chance Encounter

One day in March 2010, I was leaving the gym on my way to give a guitar lesson. I drove by a neighborhood that I had passed many times. It was the same neighborhood where Cheryl used to live with her parents. For some reason, I still remembered their neighborhood from the church singles days.

I first met Cheryl through her older sister, Heather, at our church singles class. I had seen Cheryl around the class before but didn't know who she was. I remember that my first impression of Cheryl was that, aside from being really cute, she was a very "artsy" person and she *always* wore a fanny pack. It was before I began playing guitar, so I couldn't relate to the artsy world at all back then.

However, as I drove past her old neighborhood this time, a thought hit me out of the blue. It had been about ten years since I had seen or heard from Cheryl because we lost touch when she moved to L.A. I didn't even know that she had moved. As I drove past the neighborhood I thought, *I wonder whatever happened to Cheryl. She's probably married with a couple of kids by now.* Well, less than three days after that "random" thought about her, I received a Facebook friend request from her. As it turns out, I had popped up as a friend of a mutual friend on her Facebook, and she happened to remember me from the church group.

Needless to say, this got my attention. I thought, *Hmm. This could have God's handwriting all over it.* I still wasn't ready to just jump in immediately because I had been burned in the past by jumping too soon, but I had a funny feeling about her from the beginning.

I initially thought she might have kids. I assumed she could have been married because her Facebook profile photo was of her and two little boys. After checking out more of her photos, I realized the boys were her nephews. I was relieved when I found out she wasn't married. As I browsed a few photos I thought, *I remember her being pretty, but I don't remember her being this pretty. Wow, this girl is hot!* So, I proceeded to check her out on Facebook to find out more about her.

Once I checked out her photos, I realized quickly she is a *really* beautiful girl with long dark hair. She's tall and thin. The more I thought about it, I realized she could be the girl in my dream where I saw the sad bride who had been waiting a long time. What *really* got my attention was learning she wrote a book called *Never the Bride.* At that point I thought, *This is either a really bad trick from the enemy, or she is my wife and I just don't know it for sure yet.*

Then, the Lord started connecting the dots for me. I thought about the connection between my dream and her appearance and her having written the book, *Never the Bride.* I thought about my Yahoo! personals experience where I thought I heard God chuckle as I deleted my profile. I thought about how she contacted me through an online social network. (That's God's irony at work!) I flashed back to my friend's dream of seeing me in Charlotte with a beautiful girl who was tall, thin, with dark hair, and how later we would have our first date together in Charlotte. I considered my prayer campaign for my wife, and how, later on, I learned that Cheryl had three guys attracting her attention while I was praying for God to keep the wrong guys away. I also mulled over the footprints in the sand and the instant download of revelation. I pondered how Cheryl and I were on opposite coasts—

appearing to be going in two different directions—but God crossed our paths in a "chance" encounter. There were many things that added up, and God reminded me of them all after she and I reconnected.

Later, Cheryl also told me that many years prior, God told her she was ready for marriage but that her husband wasn't and to pray for his preparation. This matched God telling me that I was the one who wasn't ready, not her. She was ready and waiting for me.

I also had another really cool sign. About four years before reconnecting with Cheryl, I was thinking about what I wanted in a wife and how I envisioned her. I felt prompted to make a list, divided into categories of exactly what I wanted. This was way more specific than my old list of ten things. The categories I chose were Spiritual Aspects, Emotional Aspects, Physical Aspects, Personality/Character Aspects, Mental Aspects, and Gift/Talents. In each category, I listed anywhere from seven to eighteen traits. As I reviewed the list, it was almost as if God were saying to me, "Is everything you want on the list? Chris, go ahead and put down *everything* that you want. Everything. I want to give you your heart's desire." Once I finished my list, I finalized it and presented it to God. After Cheryl and I were engaged, I shared the list I had written with her. She was *all* but one trait from the list and that trait was minor, at the bottom of the list. It was amazing that God gave me exactly what I asked for on a list of about fifty items.

Long-Distance Relationship

Once we reconnected on Facebook, we started communicating a lot through email and a few texts. In an early email to me, Cheryl mentioned that she had a "best friend" she was waiting for, to "wake up" and ask her out. In the past, that kind of response would have been intimidating and I would have backed off the desire to want to know her and pursue her. However, since I had also been through that "best friend" situation a few times, I knew that seldom do they work out like the interested party wants.

I also felt like God was in this new potential relationship with

Cheryl. I knew that, regardless of circumstances, God would work things out according to His plan in His time, especially if I didn't try to make it happen and screw it up. So, I started just getting to know her as a person while having hope in my heart that it might work out. I had faith it *would* work if it were God's will. That was my approach from the beginning—to get to know her and let God work out the details and the result. It was different from any other relationships right from the start.

When Cheryl first popped up on the radar, and especially after I got to know her more, I did not to tell her about my dream, my friend's dream, or any "signs" that the Lord seemed to show me. I just kept them to myself and, as Mary did when the Angel of the Lord spoke to her, I pondered them in my heart as I moved forward with getting to know Cheryl. I was committed to leaving the outcome of our relationship in the Lord's more than capable hands instead of trying to use these signs as ammunition to manipulate Cheryl into being with me.

In the past, if I met a girl I really wanted to pursue, I would try every way possible to win her over or get her to notice me. I have tried praying earnestly for specific people, fasting, showing a lot of interest, showing no interest and being aloof, writing her notes, giving her gifts. I've tried to sit back and let the Lord win a girl over for me but got impatient when He didn't do it. I've tried to "be a man" and go after her aggressively, but nothing I tried ever worked to get the girl.

So, this time with Cheryl, I truly made up my mind and my heart to allow God to be God, and to allow Him to bring it to pass if it was His will. I think the difference between Cheryl and the other girls I have pursued is that I really felt like God reconnected us. I just had this unusual, inner peace throughout the whole process. For once, I had *faith*, not just *hope*. At times, I almost felt like I couldn't do *anything* to blow this budding relationship, but I would have been okay if God would have ended it. It was truly a unique feeling.

One really neat advantage of getting to know someone via email or from a distance is that you get to know the person without the physical stuff getting in the way. You can fully concentrate on getting to know them as a person without their hotness clouding your judgment or causing you to ignore important red flags. Although Cheryl is smokin' hot and I'm wildly attracted to her, I was able to get to know her as a person without letting her looks cloud my judgment.

Through our correspondence, we discussed many things, such as our general views and beliefs about marriage, family, and childrearing. We discussed our views of God, His interactions with us, and how He guides us daily. We also talked about our ministry desires, goals, callings, and vision for the future. Through email, we were able to share with each other our passions and what makes us tick. For two people who weren't even dating, we covered a lot of ground, so we both knew exactly where the other stood on many important topics. I believe that it's *really* important to get to know someone on this level as much as you can *before* you actually date them.

This concept was the exact *opposite* of any other relationship that I had with a potential wife candidate. Before meeting Cheryl, the dating process usually went something like this: Chris meets some hot, cute girl. Her good looks and that initial attraction cause him to want to get to know Hot Girl better. If Chris was lucky, Hot Girl would agree to go out with him on a date. It was usually after this first date or two that either Hot Girl would not be interested in going out anymore with Chris, or there would be some serious red flags that would arise on the first date. Many times, Chris would overlook the red flags because of his attraction to Hot Girl. In the end it never worked out with Hot Girl, and Chris would be left feeling frustrated and wondering what happened. Or Chris would end up dating Hot Girl for a while until he just couldn't ignore the red flags any longer and had to break up with Hot Girl. By that time, Chris was emotionally connected to Hot Girl and it would take a while to get over her before he could move on.

Does that process sound familiar to anyone? I went through this more times than I can count. That's why this relationship with Cheryl was so refreshing. Although I thought—and still think—that she is a little Hottie, I was able to get to know her—the *real* her from emails and long, deep conversations without chemistry clouding my judgment. I'm not saying that it's wrong to be physically attracted to the person and for there to be chemistry. There had better be some, or I wouldn't recommend marrying the person. However, the looks area needs to be kept in its proper place.

It's amazing how the inner beauty of a girl affects how you see her physically. I've met a ton of "hot girls" who, once they opened their mouths to speak, didn't seem so hot anymore. I'm so blessed that I really got to know Cheryl as a person before dating her. The more I got to know the real Cheryl, the more I was convinced that we were supposed to be together.

As I really began to know her, I saw how much of a heart for God that Cheryl has and how she has a heart for people and ministry. These were huge concerns of mine any time I met someone new. She also wanted to do something big in the Kingdom of God. By "big" I mean something of lasting value and something that makes a difference in people's lives, not the desire to be famous. She also has a real, living relationship with God that is built on personal experience with Him that is lived out in her daily life with more than just lip service.

When Cheryl came out for her visit over Thanksgiving, we spent our first alone time together. In the beginning, it was awkward. I felt like I knew this person so well, and I did. Yet, we needed to spend some time in each other's physical presence and let that part of our relationship catch up with the long-distance relationship that we had already formed. As we spent more time in each other's company, we began to get more comfortable with each other. By the end of her trip to Charlotte, I knew that I would eventually end up marrying her, but she didn't know that yet!

Once I knew that I would end up marrying Cheryl, I didn't tell her or try to convince her that it was God's will. I just kept pursuing her and let God work on her heart. This time, I decided to keep my hands off the situation and allow God to convince Cheryl that we were supposed to be together. Eventually, He did, but I knew it first.

I firmly believe that guys should be the pursuers and leaders in a relationship. If the girl has to be the one chasing, pursuing, or telling the guy how serious their relationship should be, then something is usually wrong in that relationship. I'm not saying that it *never* works out that way, but it's rare. By nature, God made men to be the *pursu-ers* and women to be the *pursu-ees*. By God's design, and example, men pursue and women respond.

If a marriage relationship is supposed to be the earthly representation of Christ and the Church, then Christ gave us this example. He pursued and continually pursues a relationship with us, His Church. It is our responsibility to respond to His pursuit. Think about it. When you asked Jesus into your heart, did you go seeking Him first, or did He come after you and you responded to His advances by accepting Him?

So, the Lord showed me that Cheryl and I were supposed to be together before He showed her. It took her a little longer to see it, but once the Lord opened her eyes and she realized it, she was able to accept me. Once she did, things happened quickly. I've told many people that once she got on board, it was like we stepped on a high-speed train. We could look out the windows and see the landscape fly by, but we were calm and just enjoyed the ride. It truly felt like another force was moving our relationship forward at a speed neither one of us could change. We felt peace the whole time, and we weren't afraid. This, my friends, is what it feels like to be in a God-ordained relationship. It has been an incredible ride and still continues to be to this day. It almost feels like we are the actors in a story that God has written, and all we have to do is say our lines and act out our parts.

What Ladies Need to Look for in a Guy

I want to share some things with the ladies. I have a sister and was protective of her during her dating stage. So, let's just think of this section as well-meaning advice from a caring brother. There are some things that I've come to realize that ladies need to be able to identify in the guy who is their *one*. Keep in mind that this is just general advice. In the end, you will be responsible for choosing the person you will spend the rest of your life with.

One of the most important traits to look for in a guy is the depth of his relationship with God. The Bible gives the responsibility of being the spiritual head of the family to the guy. Guys, like it or not, this is our role. This is a huge responsibility and we should take it seriously. Ladies, I heard someone say once that you should never marry a guy you wouldn't trust and feel comfortable submitting yourself to spiritually. Let me say that again. Ladies, *never* marry a guy you wouldn't trust and feel comfortable submitting yourself to spiritually. I can't stress enough how important this one bit of advice is. I personally don't believe it's enough that the guy is a believer. He doesn't have to be perfect, but he does need to be in a real, living, growing relationship with God where he is submitted to God properly. Then, he will be in good shape to be the spiritual leader of a family. If you follow this nugget of wisdom it will save you from a difficult marriage you may regret, especially because God won't be at the center.

Another trait you want to look for in a guy is someone who is willing to make room for you in his life. Not someone who tries to change who he is or who will simply add you to his preexisting agenda, but one who will carve out a special place for only you in his life. Too many girls end up with guys who mostly see them as conquests or victories. Then the guys just incorporate them into a small corner of their lives, instead of viewing marriage as the life changing union of two people becoming one. Also, I would not recommend marrying someone who tells you that he will change who he is for you. Don't fall for that line because someone who will change for you will also change back to who he was before, once you are married.

It is also very important that a guy cherishes and treasures you. Now, I know that some guys are not overly mushy and some may have a more difficult time expressing their feelings than others. You should be able to tell if he's got that twinkle or that *wow* in his eye when he looks at you. If the twinkle is not there, I would question where his heart really is. Where your treasure is, your heart is, too. Also, make sure that he cherishes you with his *actions*, not just his words. If he tells you that he loves and cherishes you but his actions don't line up with what he says, then you need to reevaluate the relationship. Lip service is cheap.

Another characteristic to look for in a guy is someone who has a good disposition and exercises self-control. Steer clear of someone who is prone to fits of rage or extreme anger. I know that most anyone can get really irritated sometimes, but steer clear of the guy who explodes, especially if the anger is directed at you or others. Someone who cannot control himself is capable of verbal or physical abuse. The Bible tells us that one of the fruits of the Spirit is self-control, so seek a guy who walks in the Spirit. Ladies, if you are in a physically abusive relationship, get out of it—*now*. Then seek help.

Ladies, in my opinion, here is a brief list of types of guys you should steer clear from: the wishy-washy or noncommittal guys, the bad boys or dangerous guys, the guys who always have to have a girl on their arms, or the smooth, Don Juan playboy guys.

The last guy to avoid is someone who has an active addiction or vice. None of us are perfect and we are all works-in-progress, but if someone has an addiction to something then you probably don't want to get involved with him. Such things could include alcohol, drugs, gambling, or pornography. Especially these days, with things so readily available on the Internet, pornography has become a real issue. However, if someone had an issue in the past and they have dealt with it, are healed, and are walking in that healing, then you can consider that person. Don't be afraid to ask a guy that you are seriously considering dating if he has any unresolved issues or vices in his life. The last thing you want is to be totally surprised on your honeymoon with some weird stuff simply because you didn't ask.

Non-Pursuer, Noncommittal Types

Cheryl already covered what it's like to be non-pursued, yet in a close friendship with someone you like. I won't repeat what she said. My advice is, if you've been in this friendship for three to six months and it hasn't changed, it's not going to. A guy can learn what he needs to know in that time. It's healthy for a man to hang out with someone a bit and get to know her before he asks her out and starts pursuing her. If he's still wishy-washy after a time, there is either a red flag in his mind about you, or he's stalling to see if someone "better" might come along. Either way, you're risking heartache if you let yourself stay emotionally attached to him.

At this point, I want to take a moment and confess that I have been this guy to a few girls along the way simply because I wasn't sure. I thought they were great girls, but I always had a "check" in my spirit about them. I also didn't let them off the hook like I should have. So, I apologize on behalf of myself and other guys who have done this to women. I'm sorry for any confusion or heartache that I have caused anyone in this regard.

Ladies, I know how hard it is to be single for a long time and truly desire to be married. It's also really tough to weed your way through all the imitations to find the real McCoy, or in my case, the real McKay. I can assure you from personal experience that it's always best to wait on God and do things His way. He truly has your best interests and your personal welfare in mind when preparing your husband for you. As hard as it is, be patient and, under no circumstances, ever settle for second-best.

God wants you to have His best. You may have to wait longer than you want. If you are patient enough to wait on Him, I guarantee that, when He brings your guy along, it will be worth the wait. Also, if you give in too soon and settle, you may be robbing the guy who has been waiting a long time on *you* from having God's best.

Word to the Fellas

All right guys, so far I have been addressing the ladies, but this section is for you. Let's say you have some interesting women in your life that you want to get to know and possibly pursue. Now, I'm assuming you are thinking about a serious relationship you hope will lead to marriage.

If you are just playing the field, let me caution you that your actions will affect the emotional well-being of a girl that someone else will end up with. So, be careful of the seeds you sow because you will eventually reap the harvest. Now, on to the good stuff.

Men, as mentioned, our job is to pursue. *Pursue*, not coerce, manipulate, pressure, stalk, or beg. Women don't want someone who just comes and hangs around but won't get up the nerve to be direct about his intentions toward them.

Now, some of you may have a certain lady in mind that you want to get to know first, before pursuing her. This is a good idea, and I would recommend getting to know someone before asking her out on a *real* date. However, if you have been hanging out with her and getting to know her for four to six months and you still can't make up your mind, then she is probably not the right girl for you. So, be a man and let her off the hook, especially if you can tell that she is developing an interest in you. Don't tie her up emotionally, so she won't be open to meeting the right guy for her. Also, it keeps you in the clear. If you are hanging out with a "friend" that you can't decide to date or not and the girl of your dreams comes along, you'll look like a real jerk if you suddenly dump your friend to go for the new girl.

Once, I held on to an ex much longer than I should have. I dated this girl for quite a while, and I really liked her. She was very pretty, smart, funny, and fun to be around. Although I liked her and I became emotionally attached to her, there was this little part of my heart that had some reservations about her. I couldn't fully commit to being with her for the rest of my life. I let it go on *way* longer than I should have. I finally realized that I needed to man-up and break it off. I think she probably still hates me to this day—and I don't blame her. I should have ended it much sooner, when I never got the Lord's peace about the relationship. Don't make the same mistake. Do the right thing.

If you do have someone that you are truly interested in pursuing, pray, pray, and then pray. Make sure you have the Lord's peace in your heart. Once you get the green light from the Lord concerning a particular person, go for it.

When I met Cheryl, the Lord put a unique and different peace than I had ever had deep down in my heart about pursuing her. His peace helped me weather the no's that she gave me on the front end. He also brought to mind various dreams, prophecies, and words that I had received over the years concerning my wife during my pursuit of Cheryl. *All* of them pointed to her. I didn't have to try to make the prophecies fit or justify anything away that didn't match. It all lined up.

Next, let's take a look at the mechanics of what it looks like to properly pursue a marriage candidate. Once the Lord leads you to the person you should pursue, it's very important to let His voice guide you during the entire pursuit. Now, let's cover some practical things to go with the spiritual.

The Pursuit is On

Once you are ready to pursue the woman the Lord has for you and you have established a good relationship with her, be intentional about your pursuit of her. Let her know your intentions and be frank with her. Let her know that you are there, you are interested in her and that you are solid. She needs to know that you are not going to waffle back and forth or wimp out once the pursuit begins. You can start by asking her on a real, official date. Let her know you want it to be a date. This will separate you from the friends that she has that haven't made their intentions clear.

Let her know that you care about *her*, not just that you think she's hot or has a great body. Ladies need to feel special, like they are the only ones you have eyes for. Guys, it really needs to be that way for you, too. She *is* the only one you need to have eyes for. Hot girls are a dime a dozen these days, so you need to be connected to her on much more than just a physical level. Get to know her as a person. Know who she is, what she likes, what makes her tick. What are her dreams and goals? Make it about more than her looks. There will always be physically attractive women out there. None of them will complete you like "the one" that the Lord has for you. Once you are so deeply connected to your wife, there is such a comfort, confidence, and reassurance that come with that type of relationship. It's unbelievable.

Start thinking ahead and looking to see what life decisions you need to make to get ready for her, if you are not already in that position. For example, do you need to upgrade your career? Do you need to make more money to accommodate her in your life? Do you need to give up some friends or habits in your life that are not healthy? Are you willing to relocate to be with her? Once she sees that you are making room for her in your life, it will make her feel more comfortable, or possibly scare her off, depending on where she is in her thoughts toward you. Either way, it will be a good indicator of whether you two will be together. However, make sure you don't come on too strong. For example, if you guys have been hanging out for a month, you may not want to tell her you are going to buy a larger house to accommodate her stuff.

When you are pursuing her, keep in mind that you are not just inviting someone else to step into *your* dreams, *your* goals, *your* ministry, and *your* life desires. Instead, the *two* of you will come together to form a new life. You may have to let some things go. You don't have to stop being you, but just consider her and find ways to intertwine her life with yours through shared interests and goals. Also, you both may find that the Lord has something new and fresh for you to do together that you had never thought about before, such as co-writing books.

Mind Your Manners

Growing up in a Christian home, I had a great example from my dad of how to properly treat a woman. He has always been very kind and gentle with my mom. He makes her feel like a lady by carrying things for her, opening doors, and doing some chores to help her out. Thankfully, I had a great example to follow. Unfortunately, not everyone has that positive example.

As men, we should always value women by treating them with kindness, gentleness, and respect; and that goes, even if you aren't in a dating relationship. It's best never to speak harshly to them or treat them badly. Remember, guys, your words matter. Women will remember not only what you say to them, but how you say it.

Another area to keep in mind is physical or sexual boundaries while you are dating. I know some people have different boundaries when it comes to this subject, but it's of utmost importance that you both are on the same page with this topic.

I've met couples that span the gamut—ones who didn't kiss or even hold hands while they were dating, to those who did everything but technically sleep together before they were married. You need to seek God on this topic, and let Him guide you on your limits.

The most obvious boundary is there should be no sex of *any kind* before marriage. The Bible is abundantly clear on this topic. My advice is that you should never do anything that grieves the Holy Spirit or causes guilt or shame in either of you. Also, the Bible tells us three times, "Do not arouse or awaken love until it so desires." (Song of Solomon 2:7, 3:5 and 8:4.) My take is this: *Don't get too revved up before you are able to get married and do something about it.*

If you do cross that line, talk about it, pray, repent, and don't do it again. You may also need to reevaluate your relationship and where God's place has been in it. This could mean taking a break from each other—even just for a time—to refocus your heart on God.

As the guys in the pursuit, *you* should be the leader. Establish— with her input—what's acceptable and what's not, right from the beginning. Regardless of your personal convictions on this, you should *never* do anything that makes her feel uncomfortable. Neither of you should engage in any activity that could cause the other to stumble or make temptation just too strong.

Lastly, remember that she is God's daughter and you need to treat her so. You are God's son, and you need to act like it. If you always conduct yourself around her with that thought in mind, you shouldn't have a problem staying within boundaries.

It's like the Ten Commandments compared to Jesus' two commands that He gave us in Matthew 22: 37-39. He said that you can sum up the Ten Commandments by loving God with all of your heart, mind, and soul; and you should love your neighbor as yourself. If you love God with your all, He should be first in your dating relationship. You'll be able to stand firm against any temptation to disobey His direct command for sexual purity. If you love your lady as yourself, you won't violate her conscience, lead her astray, or ask her to put her relationship with you above her relationship with God.

Once You've Decided She's "The One"

So, you believe you are to *finally* be the groom. Congratulations! Once you have peace in your heart and you feel that she is on board with the two of you being together, you can start planning and looking ahead into the future. You can start to see how the two of you will combine assets, where you will live, and if you will buy a house or rent. Then you can start working on the details of how you will join your two lives after marriage. Once you both are speaking the same language, then you can start thinking about getting a ring and how you are going to propose to her.

Guys, the proposal is *very* important. You need to have a plan, and think of a creative way to propose to her that is special to you both. Trust me, she will remember how you propose to her for the rest of her life. So, take the time to plan it out, make it special, and then follow your plan.

Once you propose, I recommend you both do premarital counseling with an experienced, happily married pastor. Cheryl and I met with the pastor who married us, along with his wife. We were able to glean wisdom from their years of marriage, to start out on the right foot. We also did a joint premarital book study. So, make sure you keep the lines of communication open and that you plan and grow together.

A Few Parting Thoughts

Now I want to leave the guys with a few words of wisdom as parting thoughts about what *not* to do in your pursuit of a potential marriage candidate, at least not until after you are engaged.

Do not tell her on the first date that you are supposed to marry her. This is a surefire way to kill a budding relationship because it's coming on too strong.

Do not tell her that she may not be a Ms. much longer. Yeah, like I did in one of my emails to Cheryl right before our first date. I was pretty sure at that point that we would end up together. She told me later that comment made her jaw drop and made her feel too pressured in the beginning.

Do not tell her about all the dreams and prophetic words that you have received that point to her being "the one" for you. Don't freak her out. If you know for sure, keep that information to yourself, and let the Lord tell her that you are supposed to be together.

Do not be a wishy-washy guy. When pursuing a marriage candidate, be intentional.

Lastly, I want to leave you with probably the most profound bit of advice in my section of this book:

Don't plan a sixteen hour first date!

I just want to thank God for being so incredibly involved in every area and detail of our lives. He is truly amazing and the source of all hope, happiness, and true love. I pray, just as Cheryl and I finally did, that each of you will surrender your love lives completely to Him, and allow Him to write and direct *your* own God-written love story.

Epilogue

I (Cheryl) want to recognize that some of you reading this book may fear embracing its message. Maybe you don't know for sure if God has marriage in His plan for your future—maybe not with the surety in which I have related my conversations with God or prophecies offered through others about my future. Maybe you've been too afraid to ask Him about this sensitive subject. Maybe you've prayed about it but aren't sure you heard an answer. Maybe the only voice you hear is the voice of your own hopes for yourself. Maybe you can't get past the enemy's voice of discouragement. Maybe you're afraid to hope for God to write your love story, especially if He hasn't clearly revealed to you that it's His plan for your life.

This is where I want to encourage you to seek God wholeheartedly for a relationship where you can hear His voice. Seek prayer mentors and counselors who also hear on your behalf and will confirm or check what you feel you hear. God's Word cautions us not to quench the Spirit, but to seek confirmation for prophetic words (1 Thessalonians 5:19-21). Test what you hear, let Him help you sort out the wheat from the chaff. Then hold fast to that which is true, confirmed, and good.

God inspired me to share this message with a culture that often chooses not to wait on Him, a culture where the divorce rate is ridiculously high, for believers and nonbelievers alike.

I don't know if God has marriage for you. I do pray there is a reason you picked up this book, that it's God's message to you, so you can have hope no matter how long He takes to set up whatever He knows is best for you.

Chris and I, independently—for almost two decades before we got together—prayed the same prayers of surrendering this area to God and asking for His help. So, perhaps that's a good place to start:

surrender. I hope and pray for you there's a guy out there willing to pray the same prayer and that God can lead the two of you together.

Some people are called to the single life, like Paul says in 1 Corinthians 7. If God hasn't let you know that's your calling, then seek Him about what He has for you, one way or the other. Either way, there is an answer, but you need to seek Him to get it. I am confident that He will answer you when it's time for you to know. I love the following promise from the Lord: "You will seek me and find me when you seek me with all your heart." (Jeremiah 29:13).

God wants to be desired, romanced, sought, and pursued just like we do. So, seek Him until you find Him. Do not give up! He's worth it.

It's ironic, but waiting on God for my husband has been one of the greatest contributors for deepening my relationship with God. My passion for God has grown while trusting Him for this. He far surpasses marriage, even when God Himself pens that relationship. No one comes anywhere close to matching my affections for God; no one can or will ever take His place. God will always be my First Husband. Let's not forget that God, hands-down, personifies all the best qualities of any husband we could ever dream up for ourselves. In fact, He far exceeds them all.

In Closing

Think of it: One day, our Bridegroom, the Lord Jesus, is coming back for us. I want to live ready for that amazing day, don't you? I titled this book, *Finally the Bride*, for a reason, alluding to giving ourselves over to truly becoming the Bride of Christ, His Church, the one He returns to embrace forever.

In Matthew 25, Jesus tells the parable of the ten virgins. Five virgins wisely kept their lamps full and had oil to spare, anticipating the bridegroom's return; the other five were not ready. Running on empty, they had to leave their post at the least opportune moment to find more oil. As a result, those five missed the bridegroom. When they got back, they found the door to the wedding was closed.

If you parallel this to what we've been waiting for, we could wonder. How could they have let this happen? What self-respecting virgin who has waited her whole life for her wedding day would miss it altogether? Matthew 25:5 supplies a clue about why; it shares how it took a long time for the bridegroom to show up. We may start out well. Our lamps shine with hope, but when things take longer than we thought, we get distracted. We get lazy about refueling. We may even notice as our supply of oil dwindles, and the flame of our passion dims from a blaze to a flicker. As time goes on, we rationalize that we'll try to borrow from others what, in truth, we can only get directly from God. He has our ready supply of oil, that fullness of the Holy Spirit that keeps our lamps burning brightly.

In human terms, no matter how long the wait to be married, our groom will be worth it. How much more so with Jesus, the true Lover of our souls?

Let's consider it a joy to place our love stories in the capable hands of God, as He's the only trustworthy Matchmaker. There is no other love story in which we should want to play a role.

Acknowledgments

These acknowledgments should not be read by those who don't know me until after you've read the book. It would be like reading the last page of a novel before you experience the story. So, if you skipped ahead, just turn back now. Come on. I know you can do it.

I'm eternally grateful to all of those who've walked this road with me. To those who've heard me cry and complain, fighting against the long wait. All of your listening ears and advice—solicited or not—have meant the world to me.

I have to thank God, for taking my purple pen away and writing my love story. For putting up with me and my snarky sense of humor, and for pulling off a story so far above and beyond what I could have ever dreamed or imagined.

I want to take this chance to thank some of you who've been there for me through so much. This includes my parents, Tom & Denise McKay, my sister and brother-in-law, Heather & Chris Gebbia, to my nephew Jake (who wanted to marry me first), and my nephew Jesse (our resident comedian). Both little guys were the most competent and adorable ring bearers.

Thank you to my purple-clad bridesmaids and friends: Julie Brooks, Lisa Felten, Susan Rohrer, Jessica Kallai Romeo, Lana Shaw, and my matron of honor, Heather. My adorable flower girl, Olivia Romeo. To JoAnna Dias and my Uncle Bill Neely, for lending their extraordinary voices. To Caroline Way, for shooting and editing the "Story of Chris & Cheryl" so others could hear our amazing testimony. To Cheryl

Wilcox, who got to know me through *Never the Bride* and joined the festivities creating the most beautiful flower arrangements. Special thanks to Diane for making my purple, feathered pen.

A very special thank you to Lisa Crates, who got to be with Chris and me, photographing our engagement through our wedding day. You've given me memories to last a lifetime of scrapbooks. (By the way, that's me on the cover of this book. It's one of my bridal portraits that Lisa took a month before my wedding.)

To my aunts and uncles for making my day so special, and to my late grandmother, Marcelle, whose most treasured engagement ring I wear today as my own.

Special thanks to my new family, the Prices (Doug and Nancy, Ben and Sarah) and the Brooks (Eric, Julie, Elizabeth, Rebecca, and Jordan), who let me take over their home to have the wedding of my dreams.

Thanks to everyone who came to our wedding to support us, and those who helped get the house ready. To those who stood up on Chris's side, his band, Pastor Thom Duarte, and Pastor Jerry & Karen Poplin.

To Sandra Holcombe, for her extraordinary editing help and friendship, to Rene Gutteridge, who brought my fictional story to life in the novel form of *Never the Bride*. To all my other amazing friends and supporters with listening ears, in addition to those already mentioned: Phil & Marilyn Felten, Sheri & Matthew Enns, Phil & Dawn Fenn, Shirley Bridwell, Peggy Schmid, Sharon Fincannon, Robbie Curtis, Brenda Salmon, Kendal Tuttle, Jennifer Ahl, Laura Robbins, Lynda Jakovich, Ali Hillis, Jennifer Dornbush, Tish Dragonette, Chris Roberts, Brady & Andrea Nasfell, Nathan & Kate Scoggins, my Premise prayer group, Connie Bryson & our ladies group, and Dana Bollwerk (& her LIT Girls).

Special thanks to those who contributed their God-written love stories: SQuire Rushnell & Louise DuArt, Troy & Christina Felten, Steve & Lisa Christine, Jeremy & Mikaela Zach, and Will & Victorya Michaels Rogers.

To Jim Stovall for always believing in my writing, and Rick Eldridge for hiring me to write movies. And to Susan Rohrer for always believing *Never the Bride* must be a film and for helping me bring this story to life.

This might sound funny, but I'm grateful to all the guys who said "no" to me. It may have hurt at the time, but I know you were being led by God, whether you knew it or not. God had His hand on my life, and you were all part of the story.

And last but definitely not least: to Chris Price. The love of my life. You have changed my life in many wonderful ways, and you teach me more how to love every day by demonstrating your unfailing love for me. I am so blessed to call you my husband and my best friend. I am so glad I waited for you. I'm so grateful you prayed those same prayers of surrender to God and asked Him to write your love story. If you hadn't, we may not be together today. I can't imagine my life without you. I love you, dearly.

About the Author

Cheryl McKay has been professionally writing since 1997. Cheryl wrote the screenplay for *The Ultimate Gift*, based on Jim Stovall's novel. The award-winning film stars James Garner, Brian Dennehy, and Abigail Breslin and was released in theaters by Fox in 2007. *The Ultimate Gift* won a Crystal Heart Award at the Heartland Film Festival, received three Movieguide Nominations, winning one of the Ten Best Family Films of 2007, and won a CAMIE Award, for one of the Top Ten Films of the year. Cheryl also wrote the DVD for *Gigi: God's Little Princess*, another book adaptation based on the book by Sheila Walsh, as well as the *Wild and Wacky, Totally True Bible Stories* audio series and books with Frank Peretti. She wrote a half hour drama for teenagers about high school violence, called *Taylor's Wall*. It was produced in Los Angeles by Family Theater Productions. She wrote a script called *Greetings from the Flipside*, commissioned by Art Within, after winning a year-long fellowship. It's being novelized for B&H Publishing with Rene Gutteridge. Her screenplay, *Never the Bride*, has been adapted into a novel for Random House Publishers and was released in June 2009. It won Best Women's Fiction book at the Carol Awards/Book of the Year Awards at ACFW and was a finalist in the top three Women's Fiction books at the Inspirational Reader's Choice Awards. She also penned *The Ultimate Life*, the sequel for *The Ultimate Gift* for ReelWorks.

Visit Cheryl's Website at: **www.purplepenworks.com**
(Photo by Vincent Wallace, www.silverhillimages.com)

Visit Cheryl's Twitter: @PurplePenWorks

APPENDIX:
God-Written Love Stories

To follow is a collection of stories from real people who've found themselves in the middle of God-written love stories. I wanted to share these with you so you could see other examples of where God has done this for people, those who've surrendered the pen and let God write His romantic masterpieces on their behalves. Enjoy their journeys.

God-Winks on Sweet Love
The Story of Louise DuArt & SQuire Rushnell
by Louise DuArt

As a kid I loved all the old TV shows like *Father Knows Best, Leave It To Beaver,* and *Ozzie and Harriet.* TV moms never had a hair out of place. They rolled out of bed with their lipstick perfectly applied, wearing a crisp apron, high heels, and a string of pearls.

The TV dad always sat in his wingback chair, reading his newspaper with the children at his feet.

I wanted to be just like June Cleaver when I grew up. I would dream about crawling into our black and white Motorola and transporting myself to 485 Mapleton Drive where life was perfect.

Years later, I got married and was living what I thought to be an ideal life. My husband had a job at an advertising agency, and he even looked a little like Ozzie Nelson. We had two beautiful sons, two dogs. We even had the house with the white picket fence.

Unfortunately, life's problems can't be solved in thirty minutes like those old sitcoms. I found that out one night when the phone rang about ten o'clock. I thought it was my husband who was working late at the office, but instead the words on the other end shattered my perfect life in an instant.

"This is Santa Monica Hospital. We have your husband here. He's been stabbed in the chest."

"Is he going to live?" I asked. I braced myself for the news.

"It's only a flesh wound, but he has so much cocaine in his system we don't know if we'll be able to regulate his heart."

"Are you sure your talking about MY husband?" I cried. I had no idea that the man I was married to was living a secret life.

He survived the ordeal, but our relationship was never the same. He eventually lost his job, ran off with another woman, asked for a divorce, sued me for alimony—and won!

I swore I would never get married again. The only time I would *ever* walk down the aisle a second time would be in a movie theatre. For seven years, I lived strictly by those terms… until an amazing God Wink happened!

I was performing in an Off-Broadway show called *Dreamstuff*. Unfortunately, the reviews weren't stellar and the show was closing that night. Right before I went on stage for my last performance, there was a knock on my dressing room door. The usher handed me a card and said, "There's a man in the audience. He says he knows you and would like to see you after the show." As I read the business card, my heart leaped. "SQuire Rushnell!"

I had a major flashback. I met SQuire thirty years before. He was Vice President of Children's Television at ABC when he first saw me in a show at Madison Square Garden called *H.R. Pufnstuff*. I played the part of Witchiepoo. Later, he was working with the producers of that show to develop a Saturday morning block of programs. They had come up with the idea to create a rock group that would wrap around the ABC Saturday morning lineup. When it came to casting a comedienne, SQuire had made the suggestion to the producers that they should hire the girl who played Witchiepoo. That was my first big break in TV, and it launched a wonderful 30-year career.

Several years after that initial meeting, SQuire's marriage had broken up. He moved to Washington, D.C. where he was running a cable network. Every weekend, he would spend time with his son, Grant, who was living in New York City. He had promised him that he would take him on a long anticipated, fun-filled weekend in Canada coinciding with a meeting he had scheduled in Toronto. At the last minute, the meeting was canceled. The trip had to be called off, and his son was upset.

SQuire said, "What do you say we stay in New York and take in a Broadway musical?" Grant is developmentally challenged so it is difficult to change plans in midstream. Grant's brightness was restored when SQuire spotted Dreamstuff in the N.Y. Times theatre section and exclaimed that one of the stars was an old friend. "Hey, maybe we can meet her backstage!" They came to the theatre that night, not knowing this was the last performance of the show.

After the show, I couldn't wait to see the man who had given me my first big break in television. It would be fun to catch up. As I walked into the lobby, I looked for him through a sea of people—when suddenly our eyes met. The feeling I had was nothing short of exhilarating. I knew that instant that he would be the man that I would spend the rest of my life with. All my insecurities melted away when I looked into those gentle eyes. It was as if God's was saying, "You can trust him. He'll never hurt you. We went out for coffee that day, and we have had coffee every day since.

God's divine alignment and that extraordinary God Wink changed our lives forever. What if his trip to Canada hadn't been canceled? What if the show had closed the day before? Little did I know that God had SQuire waiting in the wings, all those years, for such a time as this.

As I finish this story, SQuire and I are sitting in front of a roaring fireplace where the snow is falling outside our home on Martha's Vineyard. It is like a picture postcard. I feel the warmth of his love next to me and I am truly blessed.

Eat your heart out, June Cleaver. You never had it this good!

THE ~~END~~ BEGINNING

Visit SQuire and Louise's websites at: whengodwinks.com, louiseduart.com, coupleswhopray.com.

Notes from a Dreamer
By Christina Felten

In 2010, I realized that I was just going through the motions. I was a school teacher at a public school. I also taught music part time and was in two different bands. My life was chaotic, stressful, and frustrating. I felt like I was living life with no goals, purpose, or motivation. I knew I wanted more. I wanted to live for something beyond my own dreams. So, I prayed that God would radically change my life. He did. I prayed for Him to show me what He wanted me to do. He did. I prayed for Him to break my heart open. He did. I prayed for clarity, direction, and purpose. He gave them to me. Not in ways I ever could have imagined. Not in my timing, but so full of goodness I couldn't dream of saying no.

I remember 2011 with gratitude and joy. Month by month, moment by moment. God swept me off my feet and left me breathless and trembling. I am humbled by our God who cares for each one of us and loves so deeply. He has given me so much more than I deserve. So, I reflect with a thankful heart.

In December 2010, just days before Christmas, I resigned from my teaching job and moved to Uganda. I decided to go for six months and then see where God led me. I celebrated Christmas with the children and staff of an orphanage for children with special needs. It opened my eyes to the plight of so many children who are living on the streets of cities around the world. The stories wrecked me.

In February, I met Mikisa for the first time. She lived on the streets of Kampala. She had been abandoned in a ditch at age two, and was suffering from severe malnutrition, malaria, and multiple physical and cognitive disabilities. I knew right away that there was something special about her.

I wanted her to have a family. I felt God speaking to me very clearly, telling me I needed to do more than just help out. I felt Him tell me I needed to show love in a real and lasting way. God wanted me to be Mikisa's mom.

At first, I didn't think adoption was a practical option for me. I resisted God's call because it didn't fit in with the plans I had for my life, but love is a powerful thing. I honestly couldn't imagine the rest of my life without this little girl in it.

As a single girl embarking on an adoption journey of a child with special needs, I accepted that having Mikisa probably would mean giving up on the idea of marriage. I didn't think I could find someone who would want both of us. I chose to adopt Mikisa anyway, even though I had always dreamed of marrying someone before having children. I felt called and knew deep down that I couldn't walk away from her. I imagined that I would be a single mom for years, possibly forever, and that it would be hard, but I also had peace and knew that God would get me through it.

In early March, I made the decision to pursue legal guardianship of Mikisa. Being Mikisa's mom has changed my heart and my life in ways that I never would have imagined possible. It's been really challenging, but also incredibly beautiful. God has shown me again and again that He is in this and He is good. This is His story. I am so blessed to have this unique and specific calling to be a mom to a little girl who has never had one.

April brought the rain and increasingly complicated aspects of adoption paperwork. Doctors told me Mikisa would never walk or talk. They said she was "retarded" and told me I was crazy to be adopting her. Our love for each other grew steadily and as her personality developed it became more and more clear why God had chosen her to be my daughter. Her adoption story is built on immense loss and pain, but also full of powerful redemption.

In May, I had to come back to the states for three weeks to complete my home study and other immigration-related paperwork. It broke my heart to leave Mikisa when she was just beginning to bond with me, but God used that time of separation to bring even more beauty and love into my life.

God brought Troy Felten into the picture at just the right time. He was a friend I had known for several years. He kept up with me from my blogs about Mikisa. I didn't realize his heart was warming toward me romantically because of what I was doing. Here I thought I would be single because of my choice to adopt Mikisa. Instead, my actions were capturing the heart of a wonderful man. God had another plan in mind!

Troy and I started dating just before my return to Uganda. Our friendship had grown more and more personal during my time in Uganda, with frequent emails back and forth and several Skype calls. Through the tough summer of attachment issues, uncertainty and waiting, our long-distance relationship provided sustenance and encouragement and so much joy.

In July, I went to court and was granted legal guardianship of Mikisa Mae. Troy was visiting when we got the verbal ruling. We were overwhelmed with gratitude and excitement.

August brought some more paperwork issues and delays with Mikisa's visa, but we eventually managed to get on a plane and move home to the States. We couldn't contain our joy.

Then, just a week after our arrival, Troy asked me to marry him. Of course, I said yes! Troy and I were married October 15th, 2011. I never dreamed I would find someone who is so perfect for me. Troy is the most amazing husband and dad. I am so incredibly blessed to have a companion to walk through life with, to shoulder these burdens with me, and to share the deep joy. It is so wonderful to be known and cherished.

In December, we celebrated Mikisa's sixth birthday. Our little girl, who had never celebrated her birthday, was showered with love. We invited her favorite people over and cooked her favorite food. She loved every minute. Then we celebrated our first Christmas together, and we experienced the wonder of the season through a new and fresh lens. The miracle of life and the promise and the hope that is found in Jesus are so much more real to us now.

The year 2011 is one we will never forget. God moved in powerful ways, and He allowed us to be part of an incredible story of His love. Love—our lives transformed because of it. So many new beginnings. Answered prayers. This is to live fully. It doesn't get sweeter than this. God has moved in our lives this year with unwavering love and faithfulness. He showed me that by letting everything go and following Him, life becomes so much better. God has plans beyond our wildest expectations.

To Follow Christina's Story, go to:
www.welcomeblessings.wordpress.com

My First and Last Blind Date
by Lisa Christine

It was a typical Monday morning when a co-worker and friend asked if I would be interested in meeting someone. I said "yes" hesitantly and Cindy proceeded to tell me about Steve, a single guy in her Sunday school class. To make the date more comfortable, Cindy and Steve's two best friends would also be in attendance.

I had spent several of my adult years praying and trying to trust God to help me enjoy Him as my Holy Spouse. In my thirties, I had been living in a couples' world much longer than I wanted or anticipated, and I did not hesitate to remind God of this fact. It was difficult to be content with the single lifestyle when deep inside, I saw myself as a Mrs. rather than a Ms.

God gently reminded me His timetable is not the same as mine.

The details of the evening were more thought out than most high school dances. To continue on the comfort theme, Steve called me the night before for a few minutes. The attire for the evening would be jeans, and Steve, the gentleman, would pay for everything. It all seemed so organized; why was I worried?

I would be meeting everyone at an unfamiliar restaurant, so I left in plenty of time. Cindy warned me it was tricky to find a space in the parking lot, and she was right. Prepared to circle the block, I came upon a one-way street, which brought me farther from the restaurant, and I ended up in a residential area, totally lost. Prior to the GPS days of present, I called Cindy, but of course she had already left. I asked God for help. Stopped at a red light, I looked in my rear view mirror and saw a familiar face: Cindy's. I let her pass and followed her to the restaurant, thanking the Lord profusely for His guidance. I had no idea what the night held, but I was now confident God wouldn't leave my side.

When I first saw Steve I thought, "Phew. This is the type of guy I could fall for." After we ate pizza, we went to a comedy club, and then had dessert at a bakery across the street. There were moments of awkward silence, times of laughter, and interesting conversation. At the end of the evening, with the three others watching, Steve shook my hand and I thanked him for a nice time.

All the way home, I had a one-sided conversation with the Lord, wondering if I had said too much or too little. I wasn't sure what Steve thought of me, nor was I sure exactly what I thought of him. I soon found out when we got together for another date the following week, this time just the two of us. We met at a park and had sandwiches, followed by a walk around the grounds, a drive around town, a game of bowling, trip to the mall, and dinner at a local fast food restaurant. Our marathon date ended with Steve giving me a quick hug.

Steve and I went on to have several dates after that. One rainy afternoon, while waiting for a traffic light to turn green, I began praying for Steve. I thanked God for him and asked the Lord to keep him safe. I also asked God for wisdom regarding our relationship. I didn't want to get my hopes up if Steve wasn't the man God had handpicked for me. I needed God's reassurance. As I arrived home a few moments later, I noticed a beautiful rainbow in the sky. I quickly ran inside, found my camera, and frantically snapped and clicked, capturing what I believed was the answer to my prayer. Seeing the rainbow in the sky, at that particular moment, filled my heart with such peace. I watched it until clouds hovered over the vibrant colors and none remained.

Ten months after being introduced to each other, Steve, on bended knee, proposed in the exact spot where we had first met. He asked if I'd share all my dates with him. I happily said "yes."

Visit Lisa's website at: writingbylisa.com

When I Wasn't Looking
by Mikaela Zach

"I am not dating anyone for the *entire* first year that I live in California!" I cried to my best friend. "I just need to focus on figuring out what I am doing here and who I am right now." I had just moved to California from Minnesota; a childhood dream finally fulfilled. I would be close to my family, had a great job, and a fresh new start. The last thing that I wanted was a boyfriend. Experiences had led me to complete exhaustion when it came to relationships. It was becoming tiring, believing someone was "the one" only to find that the relationship wasn't as wonderful as I first thought.

After years of long-term relationships, I was starting to wonder if I was ever going to find anyone. My first really serious boyfriend and I dated for about two years. We had visited jewelry stores together and talked about wedding dates. I was young, and as I started to grow into who I am today, I realized that he wasn't right for me.

Then, I found a man who fit me perfectly on paper. He was everything that I thought I wanted. We fought a bit, but hey, that was normal, right? He didn't really get along with my friends, but he was so right for me. They would all come around eventually, right? After a while I realized that if I were to marry this man (yep, we went shopping for rings, too…this one bought a diamond), I would be settling. Imagining myself on my wedding day didn't bring feelings of joy. It made me worry. So, two and a half years later, after trying to convince ourselves that we were perfect for each other, we called it quits. A few months later, I moved to California.

Once in California, I quickly became consumed with work and trying to make friends. I didn't think about finding Mr. Right. Then it happened. Funny how God seems to work His magic when we are not looking for it. When I finally just gave up and decided I wasn't going to keep watch anymore, I found my husband. Well, a friend found him for me.

It was New Year's Eve. All of my friends were going to a huge party. All but one. My friend Phil was headed to a smaller party on the way to the bigger one. I didn't really know the people throwing the smaller party, but for some reason I asked if I could go. He said sure, and we both promised that we would simply stop by, leaving after a short while to head to the other party.

At the party, I met Dana. I had heard of Dana. She was also from Minnesota, and everyone that knew us assumed we would just be instant friends because of the fact that we were from the same state. I generally rolled my eyes when anyone mentioned this, but when I finally met her, we became instant friends! We spoke for maybe 20 minutes. Then, Phil and I left. I was very excited about this solid new friend, and I was excited to talk to her again. Little did I know, something was brewing in her mind!

A few weeks later, Dana invited me to join a group on Myspace. I didn't want to be rude, as I wanted to develop a friendship with this woman, so I joined the group—and then never went to the page. A strange man contacted me a few weeks after that on Myspace. I thought he was some creepy Internet playboy who was trying to do...who knows what. So, when I got his message, I sent him a pretty snippy reply, essentially telling him to leave me alone. He responded that he was a friend of Dana's and that he had noticed I joined the group she invited me to join. He noticed one of my favorite books was one of his as well. (It was listed on my page. Oh, this is starting to sound like a junior high love story...we met on Myspace...we'll just say we met through a mutual friend!) We started talking, met in person a few weeks later, and the rest, as they say, is history.

To help things along, Dana contacted me shortly after Jeremy did to confess that after meeting me at that party, she immediately thought I would be perfect for her friend. She had created the group on Myspace and invited the two of us to join it, assuming that we would eventually talk on the page, but like I said—I never went to the page!

Jeremy and I didn't live close to each other, so she knew that we wouldn't have opportunities to meet naturally. So, she encouraged Jeremy to contact me directly. It was good she confessed, because I was feeling a little weird about meeting someone on the Internet, and was considering putting it all to rest.

God is so good. He waited until I was just spending time with Him, no longer looking for someone else to fill me, and then He brought my husband and I together, in a pretty creative way. He knew what He was doing. I had just sort of forgotten to trust Him. Had I married either of my previous long-term boyfriends, I probably would have been happy, but I wouldn't be living in God's best for me. It was so worth the wait!

Royalty in Waiting
by Victorya Michaels Rogers

I was only five years old when I began scanning the horizon for Prince Charming. Every fairy tale my mother read to me at bedtime became my own story. In my mind, I was Cinderella, Snow White, and the Beauty whose love turned the Beast into a Prince. As I got older, I realized that what I really wanted was the kind of love my parents had. After years of marriage and raising three children, they still held hands in an amusement park, and kissed after riding the roller coaster. They always made love look so easy.

It never came easy for me. In high school and college, I was every guy's best buddy, not the girl they asked out on Friday night. All my romance stemmed from a rich fantasy life, which was probably what drew me to Hollywood.

While, as a talent agent, I enjoyed meeting Brad Pitt, Don Johnson, and Kevin Costner, it occurred to me that I needed to be taking my cues from the actresses. I studied the way they walked, talked, dressed, and how they handled relationships. I also read every self-help book on the market. Then I put everything I learned into practice, refusing to exploit my sexuality.

I went from wallflower to the belle of the ball overnight. I not only learned to get that all-important first date, I could keep them coming back for more. I was pursued by a Grammy Award-winning rock star, an Academy Award-winning actor, and a top country singer. I dated men of all professions and personalities including a pro-golfer, a pilot, various businessmen, policemen, firemen, a producer, a concert promoter, a model, and a financial planner.

But I was no closer to walking down the aisle.

In fact, my heart felt so bruised and broken, I wondered if even God could put all the pieces back together again. I was weary of dating men whose values differed from my own, but finding a Christian man in Hollywood seemed like finding a pearl in a sea of oysters.

My drive-on pass allowed me to park on the Paramount Lot where two of my clients were working on a new movie. I checked on my clients before stopping by the Craft Services table for a snack. The star of the movie, an Academy Award-winning actor I knew, sidled up next to me.

"Why didn't you return my phone call?" he asked.

"It's pilot season, and I've been swamped," I said.

"*Action!*" the director bellowed, cutting our conversation short. He stepped onto the set as cameras rolled, and I figured it was a good time to leave. So, I did.

Ten minutes later, I was almost across the Paramount Studios lot walking to my car when I was literally run over by a bicycle. When I recovered from my shock, I realized it was *him!* He walked off the set, grabbed a messenger's bicycle, and chased me down for walking out on him!

"Why won't you go out with me?" he asked, charm dripping from every word.

I sighed. "Because I'm a good Christian girl, and you're *not* a nice guy. You're not going to change, and neither am I. It won't work."

He turned up the charm until it sizzled. I knew that being a "good girl" was the ultimate challenge for colossal egos in Hollywood. I knew that he didn't have a reputation for long-term relationships, but my emotions ran roughshod over my logic. We'd had fun together in groups, but now he wanted to go out with *me!*

The day of our date arrived. I preened and primped in front of the mirror until there was nothing more I could do.

This is going to be a date to write about! I thought, right until the moment I realized that he stood me up.

The same day we were supposed to go out, he moved in with his co-star. It was the story of my love life—all glitter and glamour without any substance. *Someday my prince will come,* I thought, but with each passing year it was becoming harder to believe. *God, do you really have a plan for my life? Does it include a husband who loves and serves you?*

It was Thanksgiving morning, and I had a migraine headache as I drove to my parent's house in Garden Grove. Obsessing over my single status and my headache, I never noticed the Highway Patrolman who followed me for four miles. I was doing 70 in a 45-mile per hour zone when he pulled me over.

"Let me see your driver's license!" he growled.

Head throbbing, I looked up at him and felt my pulse do a staccato rhythm. He was the most gorgeous man I'd ever seen. I tried charming him, but he remained surly and wrote me a ticket.

Clearly, God was too busy to handle something as small as my love life, I reasoned. Maybe with the world in crisis, the Lord needed some help. I paid the ticket, but wrote down the officer's badge number. Then I sent him a note at the precinct.

Since I know how terrible you feel about writing me a ticket on a holiday, I'll let you make it up to me by taking me to dinner — if you're single.

He accepted. I walked into the restaurant to meet him. He was even more gorgeous than I'd remembered! Over dinner, I discovered that he was funny, witty, and interesting. Ours was a whirlwind romance — until he dumped me.

He was an example of what I called Missionary Dating. Missionary dating, I reasoned, was a way to help God. You dated unbelievers in the hopes of getting them to become Christian. It never worked and always left me heartbroken.

Eventually, I met a Christian man I *knew* was the right one. Not only were we a great couple, but we worshipped together in church. *This was it! Thank you, God!*

The night I found out he'd been cheating on me, I was so devastated that I fell to the floor and couldn't get up. Sobbing uncontrollably, I crawled to the bathroom and threw up for hours. I was at the end of myself. Something was wrong, and all evidence pointed to me.

Over the next few weeks, I took a hard look at my life. Professionally, I was goal-oriented and successful, but my love life was a shambles. *Maybe I should set some goals.* My first step was to decide exactly what I wanted in a man. It took some thought and soul-searching, but I wrote a list of traits that I wanted in a husband. Looking at my list, I realized I'd been dating men who were the polar opposite of what I wanted. I wrote a Want Ad for the type of men I'd been attracting.

Wanted: Angry, irresponsible victim from unstable, alcoholic, abusive family. Must be self-absorbed and critical of every move I make.

I realized that, subconsciously, I'd been looking for a man in need. I thought rescuing someone would make him fall desperately in love with me. Yet every man I'd "fixed" left me for another woman.

What a wake-up call! Maybe instead of being mad that God hadn't let me drag one of them down the aisle, I should get down on my knees and thank him. It was a great way to start over. I prayed and made a firm decision that if I couldn't have the man of my dreams, I'd rather stay single. I knew beyond a doubt that the man on my list would have to be an answer to prayer. So each morning, I prayed over every detail of the man I hoped to marry.

As months turned into years, I focused my attention on living life fully. I got out of debt, and built a nice savings and comfortable retirement portfolio. Once a month, my single girlfriends and I took a short trip. Once a year, I fulfilled some lifelong dream — like parasailing in the French Alps.

Six years later, in 1996, dressed in a sparkly blue gown with high heels, I stepped onto the red carpet at the Golden Globe Awards held at the Beverly Hilton. Light bulbs flashed like a fireworks display as I mingled with the stars. In the lobby, my friend Cathy was talking to a man dressed in casual slacks. A businessman from Oklahoma, Will Rogers, happened to be staying in the hotel and came to the lobby to enjoy the festivities. Cathy took him backstage, where we visited for a while.

Ten months later, Will was back in town on business and called me. I was getting ready for my Saturday morning hike and invited him to come along. This time, I wore shorts and a T-shirt, no makeup and my hair in a ponytail. As we climbed up to the Hollywood sign, Will shared what his faith meant to him. He talked with enthusiasm about his goals and dreams. By the time we started back down the hill, I realized an amazing thing. Will didn't want to become a star. His ego and self-esteem were whole. His career didn't even need a boost.

Will Rogers didn't need me.

He just liked me — for me. We had so much to talk about we could hardly stop. When he flew back to Oklahoma, we emailed every day. Frequent flier miles mounted as he flew back and forth to California. Two years later, I felt like a princess walking down the aisle of the Crystal Cathedral. As Will took my hand, promising to love and cherish me, I realized that every woman should hold out for a prince — especially if her Father is the King.

Visit Victorya's site at: www.victorya.com

IF YOU ENJOYED THIS BOOK, YOU MAY ALSO ENJOY:

NEVER THE BRIDE a novel by Cheryl McKay & Rene Gutteridge / Published by Waterbrook Press

IS GOD SAYING HE'S THE ONE: Hearing from Heaven about That Man in Your Life by Susan Rohrer

THE HOLY SPIRIT: Amazing Power for Everyday People by Susan Rohrer

Coming Soon:

From the screenwriter of
The Ultimate Gift & *Never the Bride*

Finally
Fearless

Journey from
Panic to Peace

Cheryl McKay

Made in the USA
Lexington, KY
10 August 2016